Voices of

Oldham

T0347156

Voices of

Oldham

Derek J. Southall

The History Press

Frontispiece: Three little boys on the path leading to Oldham Parish Church.

First published 2005

Reprinted in 2008 by
The History Press
The Mill, Brimscombe Port,
Stroud, Gloucestershire, GL5 2QG
www.thehistorypress.co.uk

Reprinted 2010, 2011, 2012

British Library Cataloguing in Publication Data.
A catalogue record for this book is available from the British Library.

ISBN 978 0 7524 3544 2

Typesetting and origination by
Tempus Publishing Limited.
Printed in Great Britain

Contents

Acknowledgements

I would like to put on record my thanks to all those whose words and images make up this book for the unstinting and generous way in which they responded to my requests for interviews and photographs. I interviewed: Mr Brian Bardsley, Mrs Dorothy Bennett, Mrs Marian Buckley, Mr Derek Dyson, Mr Wilfred Finnegan, Mr Jack Halliwell, Mr Jim Hesketh, Mrs Marian Hesketh, Mr Ronald Hoyle, Mrs Kathleen John, Mrs Dorothy Knowles, Mr Derek Lloyd, Mrs Ella Lloyd, Mrs Isabel Lunn, Miss Winnie Maiden, Mrs Emma McDonough, Mr Stuart McDonough, Mrs Joyce Mills, Mr Michael Mills, Mrs Lily Radcliffe,, Mr Tom Richmond, Mrs Sheila Shipp, Mrs Emily Smith, Mrs Meryl Taylor, Mrs Phyllis Thomson, Mrs Mary Timms, Mrs Elsie Turner, Mr Ralph Turner, Mr William Turner, Mr Ernest Walker,. Mrs Lillian Wood.

My thanks also to the staff of Oldham Local Studies Library for their advice and practical help and for the use of some photographs from their collection.

I am also most grateful to the *Oldham Evening Chronicle* and its editor for permission to use some of their photographs, headlines and cinema, theatre and retail advertisements.

My love and thanks also to my wife, Shirley, who has uncomplainingly borne with me through all the tribulations of compiling the book.

Holidays at home in Alexandra Park.

Introduction

Memories of Oldham is my third contribution to the Tempus Oral History series, following *Voices of Ashton-under-Lyne* and *Voices of Dukinfield and Stalybridge*. It is important, from the outset, to understand how oral history differs from our usual interpretation of history. When we speak of history, we usually mean the careful researching of historical facts, which can be backed up by tangible evidence. Oral history also deals with the acquisition of facts, but from a different perspective. Its foundation is not careful research. Rather it relies on the recorded memories of people who lived through an era and are able to recall that era for the reader through those memories. We are all only too aware how memory can sometimes be imperfect. We may recall quite easily the substance of an incident, or a well-known event, or a personal experience; specific facts relating to those things may not be as easily recollected, or may be remembered imperfectly. So, if you are looking for accurate historical fact, oral history is probably not the place to find it. If, on the other hand, you want to know what it was like to live in a particular town at a particular time, as remembered by the people who lived in that place at that time, then oral history is for you. You will find in it the joy, the sadness, the highs and the lows, family events and town events, all seen through the eyes of the people whose memories are recorded. In addition, you will see through those same eyes the streets and buildings – some long vanished – of the town in which they lived, and of which they speak with much affection.

This oral history of Oldham during the first half of the twentieth century is an attempt to create a picture of this mill town (lying some eight miles to the north east of Manchester) from

Werneth Council School infants in the late 1930s.

the recollections of people who were born in Oldham and lived there during that period. At that time Oldham was part of Lancashire; since the 1970s it has been the Metropolitan Borough of Oldham, part of Greater Manchester.

I have put my book together from tape-recorded interviews, conducted over a period of fifteen months with more than thirty people who were born in Oldham in the first half of the last century. The oldest of them were in their nineties. Many of them have lived in Oldham all their lives. In order to interview them, I visited them in their homes, where I was, on every occasion, very warmly welcomed. Once the interviews were completed, I transcribed each one; then, from the transcriptions, I selected those parts of the interviews, which I felt fitted my purpose most effectively; it was those which I used to compile my book. If I may be allowed, I would like to record here that conducting the interviews was a most pleasurable part of compiling the book. The people to whom I spoke were invariably interesting; they spoke freely, and what they had to say was, without exception, quite fascinating. Indeed, it was sometimes only the fact that a ninety-minute tape ran out that brought an interview to its conclusion.

I would like here to thank all those whom I interviewed for welcoming me into their homes, and for their willingness to talk about their lives and to share with me, and, ultimately, with a much wider audience, their memories, even those which were sad and sometimes painful.

The memories of the Oldham people that make up this book are illustrated by many photographs, which, in one way, give the book its heart. A large number of these photographs were loaned to me by the interviewees, who kindly gave me permission to use them in the book. The photographs, many of them of family members, were invaluable in giving the book the personal touch that oral history needs to make it come alive. I am grateful to all those who kindly loaned me their photographs. I know how precious they are and how much you treasure them.

It is my hope that the picture of life in Oldham, which is recreated in these pages, is a true reflection of the time to which it relates, as well as an accurate transcription of what was told to me. I have tried, as far as possible, to use the words of those whom I interviewed, though a word or two may have been altered or inserted or omitted by me for the sake of clarity. While my book is entitled *Voices of Oldham* you will find reminiscences from people in Chadderton, Lees, Shaw, Royton, Waterhead, Moorside and so on, all places which were once regarded as part of Oldham.

When I came to live in the north-west of England in 1959, I made my home in Ashton-under-Lyne, where it still is. However, I have always been a cinema buff, and I quickly discovered that Oldham had many cinemas, especially on Union Street. It was those cinemas which gave me my first acquaintance with Oldham and its people, and which has led to *Voices of Oldham*. I visit the town regularly and have always found the people to be very friendly and down to earth. It is my sincere hope that this book is a fitting tribute to Oldham, their home-town. My book is dedicated to them, especially to GSC, whose support and encouragement helped me through the rough patches.

one

Childhood

A wartime birth

I was born on 3 October in 1914 – no, I didn't start the First World War! I lived on Hawksley Street. My mother had seven children. The first was born in 1902, the second in 1904. Then there were three children I never knew; they all died in infancy, two from diphtheria, which I believe was rife then. Then there was me, and then another sister. Our house on Hawksley Street was a four-roomed house. We had a coal fire – no gas, no electricity. We had an outdoor toilet, which at one time was a can, which they used to come round and empty at midnight. Later we had a water closet and a tippler. When water went down the sink, it went into the tippler, which tippled over every so often. There was no bathroom. We heated water on the fire. My parents were very, very poor and everything was absolutely basic. We had lino on the kitchen floor, which we used to mop, but there was no lino upstairs. My father was a labourer, who worked outdoors; he got about eighteen shillings a week. My mother was very talented; she was a dressmaker. I never had a new coat until I was seventeen. Someone would give her an old coat; she would unpick it, wash it, turn it and make me a coat from it. She was also a very good cook. She lived until she was ninety.

Mary Timms

How wrong can you be?

I was born at 677 Ripponden Road, Moorside on 17 September 1914. I was born a demic. There were no midwives in those days; there were ladies of the village who came and delivered babies, and laid out the dead. The woman who delivered me said to my mother, 'Don't bother about that one. Just throw it away. You'll never rear it'. My mother said, 'Just watch me'. She was that kind of lady. I had no proper bones in my arms and no

proper bones in my legs. My dad used to carry me about. I didn't start walking till I was four years of age. My other four siblings are all dead and gone now ... and I'm still here!

Ronald Hoyle

Pinchback and the gamblers

At the bottom of Hawksley Street was a croft – a piece of open ground. They called it Pinchback, a rather derogatory name – 'Ooh, she lives on Pinchback!' Actually it was Pinchbeck, the name of the man who owned the land. Every Sunday afternoon there'd be a gang of men come, and they'd play 'tossing'. They'd toss coins. They were gambling, but they'd be no trouble. Then the police used to come. They'd run in the houses to try to catch the men, but the people used to help the men get away. I didn't see it very often because I was in Sunday school. Everybody was very poor. I can remember waking at six o'clock in the morning and you could hear the mill-workers' clogs clattering on the cobbles of the road; we were surrounded by mills, which used to be all lit up. I loved that.

Mary Timms

Disappearing muffins

I was born in 1926 and as a child I lived at No. 20 Back Scott Street; it was a corner house. My father was a very sickly man and we were very poor. We had a tick book for the shop. Every time you went to the shop you had to take this little book and they would jot down what you had bought. It was totted up at the end of the week and you paid for it all. My mum had a hard life. She was a good mother and she must have made many sacrifices for us. She loved us, and that was all we had. It was only as I was getting older that I realised the things we didn't have; yet we didn't miss them. We didn't miss out

Mrs Lily Spencer and her daughter Emily (Smith) in front of their house on Back Scott Street.

on the important things. My mother loved baking. She made all our bread and muffins. She used to make muffins and she'd put them outside the door to cool. More often than not they would disappear. My mum didn't bother. There were so many people who were starving. She knew it was the children and that they would eat them with no butter on. They were our neighbours, all from big families. We never needed to lock our door and we never knew what it was to be frightened.

Emily Smith

Suffer the little children

When I was a child I had one pair of shoes, which was for Sundays. When I was at Hollins School, they wouldn't let us wear clogs. Everyday, when I came home from school, I immediately had to put my clogs on. I couldn't play out in my posh. I'd go to a little mission. My mother told me it was formed because they wouldn't let children in clogs go into the main church. It was very high church. Some men came out of the church because they wouldn't let children wear clogs. They could go to the day school belonging to the church wearing clogs. The men set up this little mission. My mother said that when she was a child, the children either had clogs or bare feet.

Mary Timms

Helping dad

My father was called John Albert. At one time he had a coal round and sometimes he carried bricks for a building site. I'd get up early and go and help him, and I'd take a load of bricks down to the building site before I went to school. He might pop in the bedroom and say, 'Come on, lad. We'll do a load of coal before you go to school'.

We were five children and we slept in one bedroom; nobody thought about it then. I had an aunty who made confectionery and an uncle who made ice-cream. Saturday morning was busy and they would ask me to go and grease the tins and roll the muffins and teacakes. I always had lunch with them – always brisket. They used to pay me. I did papers as well. When my uncle bought a pony, he was a bit frisky for his ice-cream cart; he asked if I would go round with him and hold the pony's head while the children were at the ice-cream cart. I got 6d for that. I was never short of money, but I earned it. I gave them their money's worth.

Ronald Hoyle

'Where does she get it from?'

I was born in 1918 at home in Webster Street, off Ashton Road. I had one brother, three years older than me. We moved a lot. I had a happy childhood. My brother was very quiet, but I was always swearing. My mother and father, they weren't swearers. They used to say, 'I don't know where she gets it from!'

Lillian Wood

Living at grandma's

I was born at 25 Howard Street, Waterhead, in 1922. I had a brother and a sister. My mother had three children in two and a half years. She always said it was worse than having triplets, struggling with three babies. But she did very well for us. She lived till she was eighty-seven, a grand old lady. I lived in my grandmother's fish and chip shop – Mrs McKay's chippy – when I was a child. The chip shop had been a public house before it was a chip shop. My mother and father got a little house, one-up and one-down, and they could only take two of us children so they left me with my grandma. I lived at the chippy, and every morning I used to go up to my mother. They had two double beds, one for my mother and father, one for the two children, in the same room. My brother and sister thought I was privileged, because they had to have half an egg for their breakfast, when I had already had a whole one at my grandma's. My grandad died in 1925, when I was three. I can remember his funeral and the horses with plumes on coming up Howard Street, a very steep street. My grandmother bought me a black felt hat, although I was only three. The shop was shut when grandad died. I can remember them bringing him into the chip shop, in his coffin, and putting the coffin on top of the counter. My grandma took me with her to sprinkle – I think it was – lavender water. She lifted me up to see grandad. I lived with grandma until I

was fourteen and started work. Then I had to go back to my mother because she needed my wage, although it was only ten shillings. Even then I still slept at grandma's.

Emma McDonough

Nobody will find it there!

When I was a child in the 1920s we had coal fires; they kept the coal in the cellar. One day I was down in the cellar with my mother, and I said, 'Hey, look here!' 'You what?' she said. Then she exclaimed, 'You flamer! I might have known you'd find it'. She had hidden some money in the coal cellar.

Lillian Wood

Helping mother make ends meet

I was born in 1924. My father died when I was four years old. By then I had two younger sisters. Mother had a widow's pension to live on. She used to do all her own baking, never bought any bread. She made plain muffins and currant muffins and sold them for a bit of money. There was a butcher's shop on Manchester Street. She washed and ironed the butcher's two overalls and he gave her 1s 6d for doing that. Also he would take a paper and go in the window and put some roast pork and a pig's head on it for us. My sisters and I had a very happy childhood, one that I still cherish. My mother got up with us and she went to bed with us. She was a remarkable lady, who always made us happy. I used to earn lots of money for my mother running errands. I might get only a halfpenny or a penny, but it all mounted up. One night I came home with eleven and a half pence; that was a record. You could buy a large loaf then for 4d, a half pound of butter for 4d. Down Manchester Street, a stone's throw from the Town Hall, there was a lot of little narrow streets. They'd no gas or electric. Some of the people had

Mrs Ellen Finnegan, Wilfred's mum.

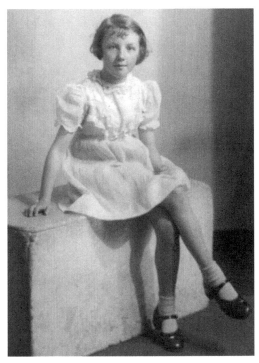

Dorothy Marshall (Knowles) aged nine. Was this innocent one of the children who teased Mr Griffiths?

very beautiful oil lamps. At the back of King's Street there was a second hand shop on the corner. They sold lamp oil. I used to go and collect people's bottles and go for their lamp oil. Some would have a pint, some a half-pint. I'd get a halfpenny for each one and it all mounted up. I used to go for groceries for other people. I would always go to the Co-op. My mother was a member. On those days you got dividends at the Co-op, two shillings in the pound. So I would get people what they wanted, at the Co-op if I could, and on my mother's dividend number – 822 – so that my mother got the dividend.

Wilfred Finnegan

Teasing Mr Griffiths

When I was born, in 1932, my mother, who came from Harpurhey originally, was living in a rented room in Retiro Street, in the centre of Oldham. She eventually got a council house in Derker, but exchanged for a rented house on Robson Street, back in the town centre. There were a lot of children on Robson Street. There was a family called Senior, who had four boys; across the road the Jennings had one boy, and so did the Scholes. At the bottom of Robson Street there was a shop, which was a toffee shop and everything. The shop was owned by Mr Griffiths. Jimmy Scholes and Raymond Jennings were absolutely terrible, but they were fun. Mr Griffiths had bow legs. They would knock on his door and he'd come out waving his stick. They would run through his legs from the back. We'd all be hysterical, but it was unkind and our mothers would come out and drag us all in. The boys also used to tie door knockers together and then knock on the doors and watch what hap-

Marian Hamer (Buckley) aged six, with her mum and dad.

pened when people came to open the doors. They were awful, really, but we would all sit there laughing.

Dorothy Knowles

'This lot now have nothing on us!'

When I was about eight we came to live on Oldham Edge, near the old bus garage. The army was there, because the war was on. We were devils. This lot now have nothing on us! The buses eventually stopped using the garage and the army took it over. They also used to use the drill hall on Henshaw Street. They put all these flags – Union Jacks, full sized ones – and plastic explosives in the old bus garage. There used to be a place on Oldham Edge that they used to call Hill 60. It ran for about a hundred yards. On top it were flat. We got all these flags and we nailed them to posts and stuck them all around Hill 60; it looked just like the Olympic Games. The plastic explosive we used like plasticine; we didn't know what it was. There was another place down Featherstall Road where they used to store parachutes. They used to have them in big silver containers, with wire around the top. We used to run across Hill 60 with these parachutes and jump off the end. I used to go about with a lad called Dougie Pemberton. Up Higginshaw Road there were a fellow called Tom Bolton, who used to grow all his own vegetables and sell them on Oldham market. He also used to breed budgerigars, poll parrots, mynah birds, chickens and pigeons, which he kept in a bird house. One day me and Dougie Pemb decided we weren't going to go to school. We went into Tom Bolton's bird house and let all the budgies and pigeons out. Everybody was running over Oldham Edge with their coats, trying to catch them.

William Turner

Two girls

I can remember playing with a top in the street, near the little shop. There used to be two girls coming home from work. I couldn't always get the top going, and they used to start it for me, so that I could carry on. I don't know their names, but there were two other girls, a little bit older than me, who used to take me to school, Doris Henthorn and Irene Hoyle. Because my mum was working in the shop, they used to take me up to school.

Marian Buckley

A very nice neighbourhood

When I was about four, we went to live on Beever Street; that's Rhodes Bank way. The street leads from Rhodes Bank up to Egerton Street; we could see the Blue Coat School. It was a very nice neighbourhood. None of

Alan Bickerton and Dorothy Darbyshire (Bennett) in the yard at the back of 99 Beever Street.

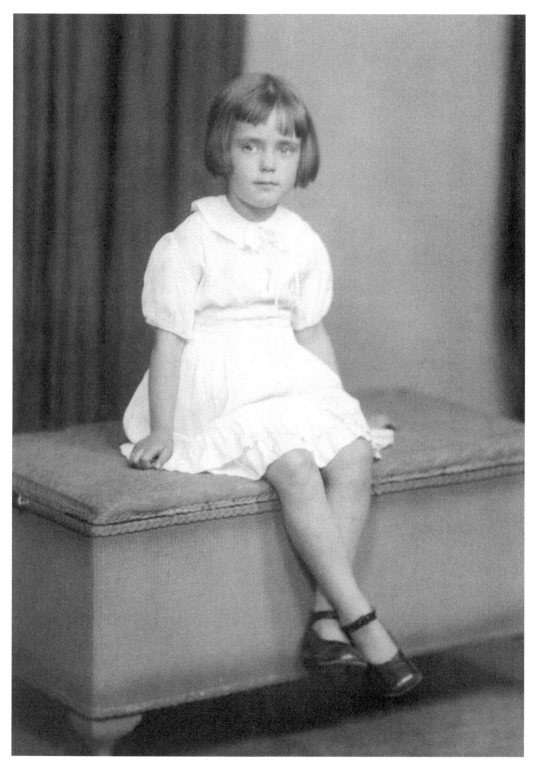

Dorothy Darbyshire (Bennett) aged six, given a penny as bribe to sit still.

us had any money, but everybody was very friendly. If you needed people, they were always there. Our next-door neighbour was a policeman. He used to go on duty and his wife would encourage me to go into their house because they had no children. She used to play the piano; she started me off with nursery rhymes and went on to 'Waltzing in the Clouds'. Her husband was a police sergeant in Oldham, six feet something. He used to look massive to me.

Dorothy Bennett

The 'Big Bump'

When I was about five, we had to move from Morris Street to Abbey Hills Road, No. 208, to look after my grandad, because grandma had died. There was no estate then, just the road. There were no buildings beyond Abbey Hills Road, just open fields. On Manor Road the ground slopes away. I used to sledge there.

We called it the 'Big Bump'. You'd take your sledge along, let it go, and it shot straight down and over the hedge at the bottom. All that's gone now.

Winnie Maiden

Cat latching

When I was a child we were frightened of the local bobby. We were not aggressive; we were mischievous. I don't think we made a nuisance of ourselves, nothing more serious than going as a gang. There'd be seven or eight lads – girls used to join in as well. We'd go cat latching. We'd go down the street, after we'd been to pictures, knocking at all the door latches. If you were caught, you got a good hiding. It were only mischief, but we always used to have a right good laugh out of it.

Ralph Turner

Winnie Maiden, aged four, with her mum outside 41 Morris Street. The neighbour is cleaning the paving stones.

Dressing pegs

I was born in Chadderton on 16 July 1922. I was the oldest of five children; my sisters, Emmy, Brenda and Joan and my brother John all came after me. I was four when Emmy was born and eight when Brenda came along. We were a very poor family. Brenda got diphtheria as a child and died in hospital. She was buried in her nightdress because my parents couldn't afford to buy her a special gown. They could only afford the hearse. My mother was a weaver; she worked long hours at the Falcon Mill. My father was often unemployed, though he did work for a time on the building of Broadway. He also worked at the Platt Forge Mill in Peel Street. I had to take his dinner there sometimes and the great big furnaces and the molten metal frightened me to death. My mother was the main bread-winner. She would have a baby, have a few weeks off and then be back at work. When my sister, Emmy, was old enough to go to school, I had to see to her and take her to school. When Brenda was born, I had to take her to the baby-sitter. My mother came home for dinner. I would have to run home from school and set the table. After dinner, when my mother had gone back to work, I would have to wash up and tidy up before I went back to school. The same at tea-time. I'd have to come home from school to do jobs and after the meal I had more jobs to do. So quite often, when I went out to play, all the other kids would have organised the game and they wouldn't let me join in. So I used to spend a lot of time on my own. I was nine years old. I got used to it. I used to make things. There was a draper's shop at the corner of Broadway and Middleton Road. They used to have little sample packets of prints and they'd sell me some for a penny. I used to spend hours dressing pegs, just ordinary pegs. Because we didn't have much money I used to do errands for neighbours. I also used to mop stone steps, a horrible job to do.

Lily Radcliffe

Lily Cordwell (Radcliffe) with her sisters Emmy and Brenda.

A man to respect

When I was a child in the early 1930s we respected policeman. We weren't frightened of them. We were told by our parents that, if a policeman said 'Jump', you'd jump. You didn't give them any chance to get hold of you and you didn't argue with them.

Derek Dyson

Christening the peg rug

We were poor, but I could not have grown up in a more loving environment. Mother was at home all the time and dad was there an awful lot of the time because there was no work. I remember mother making peg rugs. She would get an old canvas sack and some

Jean, Joyce, Ernest, Bernard and Frank Walker, *c.* 1946.

old clothes. Then she'd cut the clothes into strips, maybe an inch wide and perhaps two to three inches long. These small strips of cloth were actually pegged into the canvas to make a rug, maybe four or five feet square. We used to take great pleasure in christening the rug when it was put down. We would jump on it and roll around on it. There was, of course, no floor covering in those days but the rugs my mother made.

Ernest Walker

Evan's grandmother

I was born on 21 June 1930, at home, which was No. 26 Whiteley Street. The street has gone now, but you can still see the railings of the market. I lived in Whiteley Street until they demolished all the houses, which were back to back, one-up and one-down. I had one stepbrother, Evan. We always used to go and visit Evan's grandmother, up Watersheddings,

Stuart McDonough aged six.

every week. We used to have us tea there every Wednesday, cheese and onion and home-made muffins.

Stuart McDonough

Poor, but happy

I was born in Turner Street, Lees; home was a little corner shop, where my grandparents lived. Mum and dad lived there with them because they hadn't got a house of their own. I was born in 1928, the eldest of three children – I have a brother and a sister. My parents eventually got a house in Austerlands, one-up and one-down.

After about six years we moved to Strinesdale. We had very little furniture – a bed, I suppose, and a table – and we had a handcart to move it and had to walk to Strinesdale from Austerlands. Then, when I was twelve, we came back to Waterhead. I had a very happy childhood. We were very, very poor, but there was so much love between my mother and father that we were extremely happy. My father was out of work for many years. I remember at Strinesdale he did snow-shifting, and in the summer hay-making. For that the farmer provided us with milk and eggs. There was very little food. Whatever money there was, the rent had to be paid first. My father told me that when my mother was having her third child, she was very ill, and had to spend three weeks in St Mary's Hospital in Manchester. That had to be paid for. My father had to go to court to tell them what money he had, so that the court could decide how much he could afford to pay the hospital each week. They decided he should pay 3d, not a large sum, but enormous to him because they had so little.

Ella Lloyd

Paynter Street. The open door is door of Cheetham's Heating.

Watching the blacksmith

When I was a child I lived in Paynter Street. We used to play shop, using bits of broken glass, and stones as money. One of my friend's grandads had a smithy across the road and we used to go there and watch him shoe the horses and everything. He was called Charlie Webb. I had a brother who was fifteen years older than me. The first time I remember seeing him was when he was coming home on leave. He was in uniform and he had a gun.

Elsie Turner

Childhood games

When I was a child in Schofield Street, there were lots of children and we often played out – hopscotch, skipping, marbles and dobbits. There was Joan Topping, Muriel Champlein and myself, my sister, Jean and Ruth and David Piggott; we all used to play together. The skipping ropes we used to have we got from the shop just around the corner. It was a sort of twine and it was used for deliveries and they'd let us children have it for skipping ropes. The hopscotch that we used my father got from the mill. It was off the ends of big bobbins and had a hole in the middle. We used to throw it and there was always problems if it went down the grid. We went to St Paul's church on Ashton Road. We always walked at Whitsuntide and always had new clothes. We always used to go to the same shop, Chadwick's on Manchester Road. We went there for new hats. We would have new shoes and I was always upset because I had to have sensible shoes. I wanted nice little white shoes, but I had to have brown lace-ups so they would do for the next twelve months.

Meryl Taylor

Mr and Mrs George Shoebridge (Meryl Taylor's parents) and two young friends in the back garden of 94 Schofield Street.

A reason to dance

My sister and I started dancing when we were ever so young. I was four and my sister was seventeen months younger. She was a happy child and had just started to walk at fifteen months. She was knocked down by a car at the corner of Hadfield Street and Copster Hill Road. That put her off her feet again. Then an illness knocked her back. Dr Adler said to my mother, 'There's nothing wrong with her, Lily. She's just lazy, doesn't want to be bothered walking'. He recommended taking her to a dancing troupe. Where we lived on Alton Street, right facing Ethel Street, there was a lady called Marjorie Cook, who had a dancing troupe at Oldham Co-op, on King Street. My mother took us there, literally had to carry my sister. She sat and watched the children dancing. Mother said, 'See, if you don't get up and walk, you'll never do what these kids are doing'. My sister, suddenly one day, got up and walked across the room.

Meryl Taylor

Grandma's roasted potatoes

I was born at 328 Rochdale Road and lived there till I was ten. My best mate, Arthur Buckley, lived next door at 330. The couple at 336, Mr and Mrs Porter, looked after me while my mother and father went out to work. At the back of the street it was all fields where we used to play and get up to all sorts of tricks. My father's mother and father lived in Hobson Street in Oldham, which was off Union Street. My parents used to take me there on a Sunday. Grandma Bardsley had an old oven – a fire, a place for boiling water and an oven at the other side. She always had roasted potatoes in there. It was a regular thing, every Sunday. I had to go and see grandad and grandma, whether I wanted to or not.

Brian Bardsley

'Marian's been in'

I lived in Belgrave Road, Oldham, from when I was born in 1931 until I got married. I had three sisters, Shirley, Linda and Janet. My father, a model-maker, loved to make boats, but they all had to be given to the boys next door. We played with the children on our street. We had the two boys next door and there were two boys higher up the street. No-one ever locked their doors. I used to put my shoes on their stairs and wear their clogs. Their mother would say, 'I see Marian's been in; her shoes are here!'

Marian Hesketh

Meryl Shoebridge (Taylor) and her sister Jean in The Merrymakers, at Oldham Co-op.

Dressing my dolls

My mother was good at all kinds of handi-work – knitting, needlework, crochet and eventually sewing. A lady who was a tailoress came to live next door but one when I was a little girl. Mum learned sewing from her; when she had a particular piece of clothing to make, she would invite mum in to watch her. Mum would do the identical thing on a pattern. Then she would come home and do the same thing. Mum made all my dresses. They were all made up from somebody's old trousers. Whatever mum made, she would encourage me to make for my dolls. Later I made all my husband's suits when he led Max Jaffa's orchestra at Scarborough.

Joyce Mills

My first telephone call

When I was a child in the 1930s I made my first telephone call. Hanson Street came off the main road, then turned slightly and became Hillside Avenue. At the top of Hillside Avenue was a telephone box. On the turn was a bread shop. Behind our row of houses there was a church. One afternoon we could see and smell smoke coming from the roof of the church. It was my job to run up the street, go in the telephone box and dial 999. It was the very first time I'd ever been on my own to telephone anybody, and my hands were shaking. But the fire brigade came and got the fire out.

Joyce Mills

Above: Phyllis Bancroft (Thomson) aged three.

Left: Marian Knowles (Hesketh) aged seven.

'What a lovely dolly'

I lived in Werneth as a child. There were just a few shops there, opposite the police station and the fire station. There was a greengrocer next door to us and a baker on the other side, a waterman and two public houses. When bananas first came to this country, I must have been the first child in Werneth to have one. The Martins, who had the greengrocer's shop next door, gave me one. I took the banana to school, totally fascinated by it. I kept it in my hand all morning till it became completely soft. When I tried to get into it, it all squashed out. During the war we had no toys. One of my uncles, who was a wood-turner, made us a scooter. I had an old tin pram, but nothing to put in it – unless I put in a sheep's head. I did that one day and an old lady came along and said, 'What a lovely pram! And what a lovely dolly!' Then she saw the sheep's head and was taken aback. Being a butcher's daughter, a sheep's head was nothing to me.

Phyllis Thomson

Sheila Parsons (Shipp) in her cart in front of her grandparents' grocer's shop at the top of Barker Street.

J.G. and A. Parsons, Undertakers

I was born in 1932 and my brother, Derek in 1934. We lived in St Mary's Street till just before the war, when we moved to Whitehall Street. My dad had his own undertaking business from the age of twenty-one, and he had some houses built on Whitehall Street. One was left untaken, so we moved there. The business was J.G. and A. Parsons, Undertakers. The J.G. was my grandfather, James Griffiths Parsons and the A. my father, Arnold. Dad made all the coffins for the business and grandad did the books and used to walk in front of the funeral.

Sheila Shipp

More childhood games

When I lived in Waterloo Street, Glodwick as a child, there were lots of children around. We used to play all kinds of games. One of them was called 'ducky'. You built up a pile of stones, or half bricks. On top of this pile you placed a small stone which was called the ducky stone. One person was on and had to go and find all the others before they came back and knocked down the ducky stone. It was a kind of hide and seek and could go on for hours. We also played 'I draw a snake upon your back and somebody will tick it'. One of us had to face the wall, or a garage door, or whatever. Somebody else drew the sign of the snake with his finger on that person's back, at the same time intoning, 'I draw a snake upon your back and somebody else will tick it'. Somebody else ticked – touched – the person's back and the person turned around and

Sheila Parsons (Shipp) and her brother Derek at back of 28 Whitehall Street, *c*. 1938.

had to guess who had ticked it. If he guessed correctly, that person was on. If not, he was on. Then it became a game of hide and seek.

Michael Mills

Fireworks and swimming

When I was born, my parents lived right in the centre of Oldham, in a big square of houses facing the Pride of Erin pub. I was one of seven children. Later we moved to a council house up Derker. The estate was new at the time. Every house in the street had kids. We used to play rounders with an old tennis racquet. You could whack the ball right up the road. On Bonfire Night we would go round the doors singing for a few coppers; then we'd go to the shop and spend it. If we were lucky we got fireworks. I think it was coming up to the end of the war that corner shops gave each street a bundle of fireworks. I used to collect jamjars and take them back to the shop for halfpennies so that I could go swimming. I loved swimming. The baths were the Lower Moor baths on Shaw Road. They've gone now.

Kathleen John

Games on Main Road

I was born during the war and lived at 62 Main Road, in Westwood. My father went off to the war and I've never seen him since. There were a lot of lads and girls in the street that I played with. There wasn't much traffic in the streets in those days, so we used to play in the street and in the gardens. We played football and rally ho!, peggy and ducky-ducky, which was an old Oldham game that kids liked to play. My mother was working in the mill before I was born and after I was born she went back there. She worked there for twenty-five years as a card-tenter. From when I was born until I was two, towards the end of the war, my mother and me was on us own. Then

this stranger appeared and he finished up as my stepfather. A year or two later I gained a stepbrother.

Tom Richmond

A family treat

When I was a child, we used to get the tram from Victoria Street to West Street, near the market place in Oldham. We would go into the snack bar behind Yates' Wine Lodge for a cup of Horlicks. If mum didn't have enough money, we'd walk down Manchester Street to the butchers for a duck a'muffin – a kind of faggot. We'd share one if mum wasn't flush. Then we'd walk down Railway Road, and Arkwright Street, then Stockfield Road, because our house was at the top of Dalton Street. Our neighbours were Mr and Mrs Leigh. We thought they were rich because she didn't work and they had no children. When they had company for tea on Sunday, if they didn't eat all the blancmange, Mrs Leigh would bring it in for Emmy and me on Monday.

Lily Radcliffe

'That's not fancy dress!'

When I was a child in the early 1940s we used to go to a place behind Hill's Stores, called 'Playmates'. We used to play games after school for an hour. We all went across to Hill's Stores for a fancy dress party. We couldn't afford fancy dress and I just had one of my ordinary dresses on. The people on the door said, 'You can't come in here. You're not in fancy dress'. 'I'm a doll', I explained, and they let me in.

Kathleen John

two

Family Life

The Sunday roast

When I was a child, around the time of the First World War, we never had a roast for Sunday dinner. Well-off families did, but we never did; we were very poor. My mother used to say, 'Don't tell anybody we're only having potato pie on Sunday. I came to feel that − and it seems so stupid now! − unless you had a roast on Sunday you were poor. I remember the first time we had a roast; it was roast lamb. My mother was delighted.

Mary Timms

Looking after grandad

My first five years were spent in Morris Street in a four-roomed cottage. My grandparents on my father's side lived on Abbey Hills Road. They had the house built and it was done as

Mr James Maiden, Winnie Maiden's grandad.

they wanted. My grandma died and grandad was left alone in that large house. Someone had to look after him and so we moved from Morris Street to Abbey Hills Road when I was five. I can remember the little truck I had to help the removal. I pulled it all the way to Abbey Hills Road.

Winnie Maiden

Yorkshire ducks

As a child I liked swimming. The baths were on Union Street. Gregory's fish and chip shop was on George Street. We'd be coming home from swimming and we'd have a Yorkshire duck at Horseman's. They were made of meat in breadcrumbs and they were lovely. At Gregory's the fish and chip shop was downstairs and you had to go upstairs for meals. There was also a place called Manson's, where you went for sarsaparilla.

Lillian Wood

Living space

I was one of five children, three girls and two boys. The five of us slept in one bedroom until they passed a law in the 1920s that male and female children could not sleep in the same room. My parents bought a house higher up on the other side of Ripponden Road, near the Bull's Head pub. It had two big bedrooms and a box room. Mum and dad had the front bedroom, the girls had the other big bedroom and us two lads had the box room. My mother was a terror. I used to earn sixpences for doing various jobs and she used to put them in a little Toby jug and put it up in a cupboard on the top shelf, so I couldn't get at it. I always wanted a quarter pound block of Cadbury's chocolate. One day, when my mother was in the shop serving, I put an easy chair against that cupboard. I got up on the arm and I got half a crown (2/6d) out of the Toby jug and got my block of chocolate. My mother missed the money, of course, and I was grounded for a week. I wouldn't tell her what I took the money for, but I never took any more.

Ronald Hoyle

Family life in the 1920s

From the age of twelve I did ironing for my mother, because she took washing in. She used to do the washing, I'd do the ironing, then we'd put it in a basket and my sister would take it back. I think my mother charged people two shillings for whatever washing she did and she used to wash for three or four families. She had a tub; she would put the clothes in the tub, push the tub under the table and put a cloth over the table so you wouldn't know there was a tub underneath. She put the clothes in there to soak. Then she had a big pan on the fire to boil the clothes in. We dropped the clothes in there. In the corner of the same room there was a mangle. We had to do the mangling, and do the ironing on the table. There were no such things as ironing boards. She had a scrubbing board to do things like socks. Then people only changed their clothes once a week. You changed your underclothes on Friday and your mum washed them on Monday. You only had a bath once a week. You had to go in the kitchen and stand in the tin bath. You had to boil water to fill it. We had to put a curtain up so my father couldn't see us. 'Don't come in here', we used to shout. We were poor. My father sometimes gave us a halfpenny for sweets, perhaps once a fortnight, and we thought that was fantastic. We were glad to take bottles back and pick people's jam jars up and take them back to the shop for a copper. But we were very happy. We'd all sit round the table and play tiddlywinks. We'd all sing together. There was no such thing as television. We had a little wireless and it had an accumulator. When it needed to have the accumulator charged, we had to take it down to a shop on Huddersfield Road. It cost a penny, but, if my mother needed the penny for the gas meter, we couldn't have the accumulator recharged. We used to have an oil lamp. When they put the gas in, they called the gas lamps 'lazy betties'. You had to put a mantle on them. If you broke the mantle it cost money to buy a new one. My brother used to throw things about, and he often broke the mantle.

Emma McDonough

Helping dad out

My father was out of work for long periods of time. He decided to start a firewood business. He got a pen in Chadderton and I had to go on Saturdays, and sometimes Sundays, to

Mr Peter Cordwell, Lily Radcliffe's dad, with his wife Rose.

chop and bundle firewood. It was in the 1930s and I'd be ten or eleven. There was a fire and he lost everything. He bought another lorry and decided to sell coal as well. I had to go round collecting the coal money on Fridays and Saturdays. I had to go on the bus. He gave me the outlying districts while he went in his lorry to the closer ones. We had to do as we were told; in those days we obeyed our parents. One day my father said the owner of the local cycle shop wanted to see me. I thought I was in bother, but the cycle-shop owner showed me a bike and said, 'That's for you'. It was a new bike that my father had bought me. After that I used to go collecting the coal money on my bike and, even better, I joined a cycle club.

Lily Radcliffe

Blame and punishment

When we were kids, if our Ted did anything wrong, I used to get the blame from my father. I used to have to go upstairs to bed. So I used to open the window, slide down the drainpipe and bugger off up Oldham Edge somewhere. I got the blame because I were the oldest. When I lived in Limeside there were a lad called Jimmy Metcalf. In those days a pound went a very long way. Jimmy Metcalf swiped one pound off his eldest brother and he got twenty Capstan Full Strength cigarettes – swiped them an' all – and we went and spent the pound. We went to an air-raid shelter and put all this food on the bunk – apples, oranges, pears, all sorts. We left it and went back at night to get all the stuff. There were a copper at one side, a copper at t'other; they'd seen us going in. They took us to police station and asked us where we lived. My father came down and got me. He fastened me to the bed and gave me buckle end of his belt. My grandma was banging on door, 'If you kill him, I'll kill you'. But I never did owt wrong after that.

William Turner

William Turner and his younger brother Teddy.

We were all the same

My father was an engineering labourer and was unemployed a great deal in the thirties. There wasn't much work for anyone then. I had two brothers and two sisters. Seven of us lived in a two-bedroomed house. My eldest sister slept in the back bedroom, the rest of us in the front bedroom, where there were two double beds, one single bed and a cot. Everyone was alike. All the kids in my class came from families of seven, eight or more. We were poor, but there were people a damn sight poorer than us. We were one of the first in the street to have a radio. People used to come and sit on the step to listen to that radio.

Derek Dyson

Mending the pot

I remember a dreadful calamity when I was a small boy. I had two sisters, Jean and Joyce. Jean came home one day in the depth of winter. Mother had made dough for bread. She put it in front of the fire to allow it to rise. Jean was sitting there. She had dreadful chilblains. Because it was so cold she was warming her feet in front of the fire. He foot slipped, and knocked over the earthenware pit containing the dough. The pot broke and I can remember all the dough oozing out. Mother retrieved the dough, but had a problem about what to do to mend this marvellous earthenware pot. It had broken into two halves. Mother was able to repair it with an old woollen scarf. She made flour and water paste and she stuck the pot together, using the scarf to hold it till it set. We had that pot for many, many years after that.

Ernest Walker

Neighbours

As a child I lived with my mum and dad on Back Scott Street. My parents originally had six children, but two died in infancy. When I was two, my brother, who was fourteen, died. Two sisters and I survived. We lived in that little house which had flag floors. In the middle of the street there was a little passageway; you had to go up there to get to the toilets. There were three toilets, which we shared with all the neighbours. In winter you had to put your coat on and take a torch if you went to the toilet. My mum was Lily and my dad was Spencer. The people in the street were all good neighbours and looked after each other.

We never needed to lock the door. We didn't know what it was to be frightened. We kids all played together. When it was raining we went in each other's houses. 'You come in my house today, and I'll come in yours next time'.

Emily Smith

The Depression

During the slump in the 1930s nearly everybody was out of work. My mother had been widowed with three small children in 1928, so she at least had a widow's pension, not much, but some money coming in. Some poor people didn't know where their next meal was coming from. We were lucky; we had meals on the table. If you were unemployed you went on the dole. After a certain time the dole gave way to the means test. If you had a girl working in the mill and earning fifteen shillings a week, that fifteen shillings was knocked off your money. There were girls leaving home to go and live with their grandparents, so that their parents wouldn't lose money. They were really bad times.

There were not a lot of houses in our street, six or seven at most; so there weren't a lot of children. A very elderly lady, Mrs McCarron, lived next door but one to us. She had a fox terrier called Peggy. After school she would send me for a black pudding for Peggy, who would squeal with delight when I brought it back. My aunt and uncle lived in the house next door to us, and the Dabneys lived the other side. They had two boys who I used to play with.

Wilfred Finnegan

'Neighbours were neighbours…'

I can remember one very bad winter when I was a child. My dad had to go snowshifting. We used to have one of those big, old-fashioned kitchen tables. The next-door neighbour made it into a fort for my brother for Christmas. My parents were desperately short of money, and in the end they sent my brother and me around to try to try to sell raffle tickets for this fort. A few people bought them. We knocked at the door of one house and a fellow came out. We said, 'We are selling raffle tickets for this fort'. 'What's it made of?' he asked. I said, 'Wood'. Then I realised what he had actually said – 'What's it in aid of?', and I stood there laughing. He said I was being stupid and he wouldn't buy a ticket. When it came to the raffle draw, the neighbours pulled a fast one. They all knew we were very poor, and they made sure they pulled our ticket out so that my brother got his fort and my parents got a few bob. Neighbours were neighbours in those days.

Kathleen John

The most wonderful thing

When my mother was living with me, the doctor, who thought her a wonderful old lady, often came to see her. He once asked her, 'In all the years that you've lived, what do you think has been the most wonderful advance?' She was about eighty-five years old then. She said, 'Well, when we were young, there were eight families in one yard and we had one toilet between us. Now I've come to live with my daughter and we've got one each!'

Mary Timms

Above: The photograph taken for 'Meet the Mill Girl' – with Ernest Walker's family at 'high tea'.

Opposite: Mr and Mrs Arnold Walker, with their twin daughters Joyce and Jean (standing) and Joyce's friend Bill in the living room. Note the clothes airing.

'The Mill Girl'

My two sisters eventually ended up working in the mill. Joyce, being quite a pretty girl, was chosen as 'The Mill Girl'. They made a film on 'The Mill Girl', showing her way of life. They showed her getting up in the morning to go to work, dancing with her boyfriend in the local dance hall and going to Blackpool. One of the pictures had a caption which read, 'When Joyce and Jean arrive home the whole family sits down to tea. Lancashire high tea is famous in the North of England and, even in these ration days, Mrs Walker tries to provide a salmon', or something of the sort! It was all rubbish, of course. The photo, which shows the clock at six o'clock, was taken at ten o'clock at night.

My youngest brother, Bernard, was dragged out of bed in his pyjamas to have the photo taken. It was supposed to be promoting the Lancashire cotton industry.

Ernest Walker

A double tragedy

My mother's maiden name was Lily Eckersley. Her sisters were May, Alice and Doris and Jim was her brother. They lived in Hathersage Street, Werneth. Jim played in the dance band at Billington's. When their mother died, the sisters were waiting to tell Jim when he came home. He was going to Ashton on his bike to take some money to the bank, when he was killed in an accident on Bardsley Brew.

Before the police could arrive someone had stolen all the money.

Meryl Taylor

'Joyce, make me laugh'

When I was a little girl in the 1930s, my mother was very badly crippled with rheumatism. In our living room there was a lovely fireplace with an oven at one side. I remember my mother could make beautiful rice puddings in that oven. We had a square table in the middle and a carpet with a line that went all around. If my mother sat there for any length of time, she'd just stick there. Dad would have to haul her up. I was only little, but I can remember her saying, 'Joyce, make me laugh. Make me

Baby Joyce Sharples (Mills) with her mum, Hilda, and dad, Jim, in the backyard of their house on Hanson Street.

laugh'. I had to push each foot. She would be screaming her head off and I knew I was hurting her. The carpet with a line had a use. I was born with slightly clubbed feet. I had special shoes and every night I had to walk along the carpet line to get my feet straight.

Joyce Mills

'He can go now, mum'

I was born in May 1939, a few months before the war started. My father went off to join the Army. One day in 1945 a strange man came to my house and they told me it was my father. I'd never met my father, but I knew it was him because he brought me some sweets. I knew that he would bring something back for me. This very brown, sunburned chap arrived and he brought me a whole bottle of sweets, which I'd never seen in my life. After he had stayed one night I told my mum it was ok, he could go now. My father loved my mother very much. Years later, when they were in a nursing home and mum had dementia, he still called her his bride. And when mum died, he only survived her by six weeks.

Phyllis Thomson

Family life in the 1940s

My father worked on textile machinery for a long time, but in 1939 he went to work at Ferranti, on transformers. He had something to do with the instruments for submarines. He knew the Ferranti family, especially the boys. My mother had worked in the mill before she married. When, after the war, they started nurseries in the mills, and encouraged mothers, who had worked in the mill before they had their children, to go back to mill work part time, she went back. The children were picked up, but it was my job to get them dressed and ready. Mum used to work until noon each day.

Marian Hesketh

Knowles Family group in the back garden of their house on Belgrave Road. Seated: Mrs Knowles with Linda and baby Janet. Behind them: Shirley, Mr Richard Knowles (grandad) Mr Knowles, Marian (Hesketh).

An Oldham election

My father once stood for election to Oldham council, as a Conservative in St Mary's ward, because he was well known in that ward. My brother and I used to go knocking on doors canvassing for him. We got abuse from some people, but others, knowing dad from his undertaking business, were quite pleasant. On the day of the elections dad had the use of a room for some young ladies to sit in with the voters' lists. I stood outside a church – I can't remember if it was Unitarian or Moravian – on the corner of Lord Street and Prince Albert Street. I asked people their electoral number and, when I'd got about twenty, I'd run back to St Mary's Street and give my list to whoever was checking. They would cross the numbers off and dad would know who had voted. He used his car to bring people to vote and he also provided tea, cakes and sandwiches for the helpers.

Sheila Shipp

A father lost

In September 1936 my father, who had been out of work, got a job where they were working on the Odeon cinema. He was a hod carrier. The hods were big, heavy, wooden things and he was only a small man. One of the things he had to do was climb ladders with the hod on his back. When that job was finished, the men moved to where the Grand Theatre was being converted into the Gaumont cinema. The men were pulling an iron girder up on ropes, one at each end. My father was up a ladder, steadying the girder. It slipped, swung round, knocked him off the ladder, fell on him and crushed him. There was no compensation; the inquest declared it 'an act of God'. My mother got ten shillings a week pension and five shillings for me and my sister. She went back to work at the mill. We were very poor. I don't remember getting any presents at Christmas time except a water painting, and that came from the council. As a child I felt very lonely. My father had been taken away, and we moved around a lot. I do remember that my mother got £200, not from the big firm that my father worked for, but from the *Daily Herald*. If someone was killed and they had bought the *Daily Herald* that day and the family could produce that paper, they got £200. Somebody gave my mother the paper from that day and she was able to claim the money.

Derek Lloyd

Sheila Parsons (Shipp) in front of house on Whitehall Street. Note the gas lamp.

Mr Arnold Griffiths Parsons, Conservative Candidate for St Mary's Ward for Oldham Council.

Aunty and uncle Mellor

In 1933, when I was just twelve months old, my mother and I moved into No. 9 Robson Street. Everybody is moving furniture and I disappear. When it all comes out, I'm next door but one. They wondered where this child came from and must have thought, 'It'll be theirs next door but one. We'll take her in when they've finished.' From then on they were like my family. There was my aunty and my uncle Mellor and there was their eldest son, Billy. I'd have a meal at home and then go and have a meal in their house. They had a dog called Ruff. They'd send him for me. He'd push me against the wall and I'd hang on to his fur while I got to aunty Mellor's. My childhood was absolutely magical. I went into aunty Mellor's every Sunday. We used to listen to the radio. I'd sit on the table and sing all the hymns they were singing.

Dorothy Knowles

Christmas

Christmas! Wonderful! We always had the same – an orange and maybe a piece of chocolate; very little in presents. I never had a pram. I had a doll when I was a little girl and it had eyes that moved. My youngest sister poked them out. We firmly believed in Father Christmas.

Mary Timms

Christmas trees

My mother made a point that we had a Christmas tree. There wasn't many presents like there is now. We were lucky if we got presents. We always had a new penny, an orange and things like that, but not many toys. I always had a little scales and I used to play shop in a corner of the room; my mother used to give me rice, peas and everything.

Dorothy Marshall's (Knowles') uncle Mellor with his two children.

Emily Spencer (Smith) with her doll outside the house on Back Scott Street.

When I got married, being the youngest, my mother thought, 'We won't bother with Christmas trees any more'. I got the ornaments off the Christmas tree and I passed them on to my daughter.

Dorothy Bennett

Christmas presents

Christmas, when I was little in the 1920s, was lovely. We never knew what we were having, or if we were getting anything. There was no money to spare on toys, so we never thought about them. We knew Christmas was coming because of the decorations in school. They would build you up to it by rehearsing Christmas plays, decorating the classrooms and making calendars. As far as Christmas at home was concerned, you never got excited about it, about what you were going to get, because you just didn't expect anything. So, when you did get something, it was wonderful. One year – the most exciting one – I got a baby doll. It was one of the baby dolls that you see in shop windows, fully dressed. It looked real. I knew my mum didn't buy this doll because we didn't have the money ... I think my godmother bought it. This particular Christmas Day I got this big box. It was wrapped in brown paper

and string. When I saw the box, I was too excited to open it. Then I did open it and I saw the doll. That doll went everywhere with me, except school. I never took it to school. Strangely though, I never gave it a name.

Emily Smith

'She's been and defied me'

My father, I was told, once queued up for two hours at Oldham Co-op, when he found out that there were artificial Christmas trees for sale. One year, when I was ever so small, our Christmas tree was on a console type radio. My mother came to me and said, 'Are you eating the chocolates off the tree?' They used to buy chocolate that was shaped, in silver paper, like an ornament. 'No', I said. 'You have been at it; that silver paper's been nibbled'. A few days later she gave me the biggest hiding; my legs were red. My sister said, 'What are you doing?' Mum said to her, 'I told her not to eat those chocolates on the tree. She's been and defied me'. I cried and said that I hadn't touched them. When they took the tree down they found little mice droppings. A mouse had climbed up the wire. My mother had to apologise, but I'd already had the pasting!

Meryl Taylor

three

School Days

Learning a sharp lesson

I went to Busk Road School [c. 1915]; it were right at the bottom of the road, almost on Middleton Road. I liked school. It didn't do me any harm. They used the cane; I had it a few times; it taught you a little lesson and administered sense. The hurt didn't last long, but it were keen enough to make you realise you'd done something wrong.

Ralph Turner

The Three Rs

I went to Moorside School, the village school, around 1920. All we had was the three Rs – reading 'riting and 'rithmetic. There was no sport, or anything like that. I went there until I left school at fourteen. The headmaster was called Deakin – I think he must have been John Robert, because they called him John Bob. He was a great headmaster. I think he lived in Glodwick and he used to pedal a bike up and down to school. There was a funny thing about that bike, and I've never come across it before or since – it had cane rims to the tyres. He left the school just before I did. A Mrs Hoyle was in charge of the infants; her assistant was Miss Dobson. They were both absolutely wonderful with children. The infants' classes were on the ground floor and from there you moved upstairs. Sometimes a teacher would take charge of two classes instead of one. There was a Mrs Taylor, who chewed her tongue all day. She had a cane and she caned me several times, but she never cured me of anything. In the top class we had Miss Taylor; she was an old maid, getting on a bit, but she was great fun and a right good teacher. For our alphabet and mathematical problems we had what they called the Little Beecham's Book. They were free and the school got so many. They used the blackboard and we worked with slates and pencils. We had two exercise books, one for mathematics, one for dictation etc. We always had homework, for which we used our slates and pencils. If you didn't think your homework was so good, you smudged it a bit, so they couldn't tell what you'd written. One teacher called Olive Lawton used to sit me at the bottom of the class; whatever question she asked me, I could answer and I always finished up at the top of the class. The headmaster and all the teachers went to see my mum and dad because they wanted me to try for Hulme Grammar School. My parents said, quite rightly, that it was impossible. They wouldn't have been able to pay for the uniform, never mind sports kit, books and travelling.

Ronald Hoyle

Learning to spell

I was five when I started at Waterloo School on Waterloo Street [in the 1920s]. It's been pulled down now. I hated that school. I couldn't spell. We had a very severe teacher and she gave us this test. She said, 'I'm going to give you a spelling test. However many mistakes you have, you'll have the strap that many times. I had twelve mistakes and she gave me the strap on my hand twelve times. I didn't say anything when I got home – you don't go home and tell them that you can't spell, do you? But my hand was swelling up. I thought I was tough and I didn't let on, because I thought I'd get in more trouble. The following morning at breakfast my mother said, 'Use your knife properly. What's the matter with you at table this morning?' I couldn't because my hand was all swollen. I showed her my hand and said, 'Mum, I can't spell, can I? I had twelve mistakes and she gave me twelve strokes of the strap'. 'Well that won't help you to spell, will it? That's not the answer. I'm coming to school with you'. So to Waterloo School my mother went. She said to that teacher, 'If you can't teach my daughter to spell, I will. We have a dictionary at home'. Every night after that I learned to spell and I can spell, but it's no thanks to the teaching profession or to that teacher, who wore her hair up in a coil on top and didn't get on with me because I couldn't spell.

Winnie Maiden

Captain of Nansen

My parents moved me from Waterloo School to Alexandra School. I was very happy there. The headmaster was Mr Lane. I did all right with my studying and I was good at sport. The school had four houses, Shakespeare, Hereford, Arkwright and Nansen, and I was captain of Nansen.

Winnie Maiden

Making the most of school

I first went to school in 1918-19 at Moorside. We used slates. We were supposed to take a rag, so that when we'd done chalking, we could wipe it off. Sometimes we hadn't even got a bit of rag at home, so I'd spit on my sleeve and do it with that. We used to lie down in the middle of the morning and we'd just started having a drop of milk. When I went to Hollins Council School the headmaster was Mr Wood. I loved history and anything to do with writing. I was good at games and was in the netball and hockey teams. I loved running; over one hundred yards I was quite quick. If I was in a relay team, I was always the second runner, never the last. I was always a bit cocky. On my last report it says, 'Mary has been resting on her laurels; she can do much better'. Hollins School had three houses, Shakespeare, Livingstone and Elgar. I was Head of Livingstone house and I was a prefect and Head Girl in my last year. We had a wonderful music teacher, Miss Teal.

Our geography teacher was Mrs Laverack. We had a headmistress called Miss Garlick, who worshipped in Manchester Cathedral. I remember her taking us to a performance of Bach's Easter music there. I was entranced. She took us to a lot of places and we kept in touch with her long after she left.

Mary Timms

Smoking Woodbines

The school [St Patrick's] was next to St Patrick's church. I started there when I was four, in 1928, and I was there until I left school. It was always a source of trouble to me, getting ready to go to school; being sat there all the time didn't suit me. After I'd left, though, when I had to go to night school, I wished I'd paid more attention at school. The headmaster while I was there was Mr Doran. He had served in the First World War and he used to tell us stories about that war. I liked that; he'd tell us about the shelling, the trenches, the whistle blowing to go over the top, absolutely terrific; he made you feel you were there. He'd been in the Battle of the Somme and told us about that. I remember teachers called Mr Murphy, Mr Dunoon and Mrs Murphy in the senior school. One morning a friend of mine, Sam Smith, was coming to school. In those days they sold five Woodbine cigarettes for tuppence. Sam found a packet, which a workman must have dropped on his way to work. After school we got some matches and there were five of us smoking in the outside toilets. A master came in and caught us. The classrooms could be made into one big hall by pushing the partitions back. The headmaster assembled all the school. We five had to touch our toes and he came down on us with the cane. We got five strokes and felt every one of them. We never smoked Woodbines again!

Wilfred Finnegan

Celebrating Empire Day

My schooldays began in 1930, when I was four years old. I went to Scottfield Primary School and I loved it. We only had two teachers in the primary, Miss Thurber and Miss Holland. We used to have cocoa to drink in the winter. We had slates and chalk and little tin boxes with cards with numbers on. The teacher had a big brass bell, which she used to take out into the schoolyard while we were out at play. We all used to follow her because we wanted to ring the bell. It was very heavy and had a big wooden handle. But we thought it was great if we could ring it. While I was at school we used to celebrate Empire Day and St George's Day, which they don't do now. On Empire Day all the pupils were dressed in the way people of the different British Empire countries dressed and had to bring something from that country. Every year we chose one girl to be Britannia. I was about seven when it came my turn. I had this long white robe and they made me a fork. But they couldn't find me a helmet. So they borrowed one from the fire station. Can you imagine, a fireman's helmet on my little head, and it weighed a ton. I don't know how I kept my head up. I had lots of friends at school, who all lived locally; so we played together. There was Agnes Kearney, Dorothy Robinson and Joyce Greaves. I used to like English and spelling, but in the primary I didn't like sums, even with the little tin with numbers in. In the seniors they had mental arithmetic and I couldn't do that at all.

Emily Smith

Manners and the strap

I went to school at four and left at fourteen, and spent the whole time at Oldham Parish Church School on Burnley Street, at the side of Oldham market. The headmaster was Mr Beanstall, a very nice man. He always used to tell us that if we kept our hands and nails

Scottfield School: Miss Furber's class, c. 1931-32.

Schoolchildren on Empire Day.

clean, shoes polished, always said 'Mr' and 'Mrs' and 'thank you', we would be all right. He used to say, 'When you shake hands with someone, you never know whether you are shaking hands with the next Lord Mayor of Oldham'. The head teacher of the infants' school was Mrs Dearden, who was also very nice. We had a teacher called Mr Sharrocks, who used to take us for rugby. He used to make us play in the schoolyard and we had to tackle proper. One of the teachers was Miss Jagger, a big stout woman. She was a teacher, and a mother as well. If anyone went to school with his pants torn, she would mend them. I can't say I liked school, but I wasn't very clever. They used to send me cleaning cupboards when there were any exams. The headmaster, Mr Beanstall, had a strap with a handle on and three leather tails. You never got the strap unless you'd done something wrong. If I went home and told my mother I'd had the strap, she ask, 'What did you do wrong?'

Stuart McDonough

Learning to be a housewife

I only went to one school, Waterhead Parish Church School, from 1926 to 1940. The head teacher was Mr Coates. We also had Miss Hayes and Mrs Waddington, nice teachers; I liked them. I enjoyed school and liked house-wifery best. We went to a big house and we did all the work at this house – the washing, the ironing, the cooking etc. We went there for three months instead of going to school. I got top marks there and they gave me a handbag.

Emma McDonough

St Luke's Infants' School, class 2, 1928. Back row, extreme left: Mrs Holt, Headmaster Mr Young. Extreme right: Miss Marson. Front row, centre: Lily Cordwell (Radcliffe).

Saying 'scissors'

I started school at St Luke's School in 1927, when I was five and went there till I transferred to North Chadderton Girls' School at the age of ten. Miss Holt, the headmistress of St Luke's Junior School, was very strict. I once used the word 'scissors', but I must have said 'thissors'. She had me out in front of the class saying 'scissors', 'scissors'. Mr Young was the headmaster; he was nice. There was Miss Whatmore, Miss Garside, and Miss Aspinall – she was strict.

Lily Radcliffe

More than a teacher

The head at North Chadderton Girls [in the 1930s] was Miss Lucas; I got on very well with her. Miss Kershaw was my form mistress right through the school. The art teacher was Miss Jagger. We didn't have much money, and if we needed things for school, I couldn't always have them. Miss Jagger knew how I was fixed and she would find bits and bobs for me. Miss Settle, the needlework teacher, did the same. She would find material so that I was able to make something. Those two teachers were very good to me.

Lily Radcliffe

'It's time for a rest, children'

In 1935, when I was just four, I started at Alexandra Road School, which was very near to where I lived. The head teacher in the infants' school was Miss Gartside and there was another teacher called Miss Broadbent. I loved school, especially reading, stories and painting, because I had read a lot at home before I started school. But I didn't like sewing.

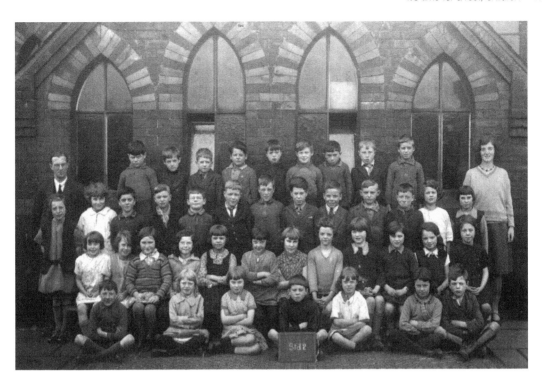

Above: St. Luke's Juniors, 1930. On the left is the Headmaster Mr Young, on the right is teacher Miss Deighton.

Right: North Chadderton Girls' School, cover for the school magazine, designed by Lily Cordwell (Radcliffe).

Alexandra Road School, class 3A, 1939. Marian Knowles (Hesketh) is to the right of the girl with the board.

Alexandra Road School, Junior 1, 1939. The Headmaster is Mr Lane, the teacher is Mrs Mills.

All we ever did was have a needle threaded with thick wool and do a line of hemming on a white sheet. We all used to have a sleep on a bed. The beds were like stretchers, all piled up in the room. They put the beds down after lunch and all the children had a sleep. If you didn't go to sleep, you had to lie quiet. I passed the eleven plus but I wasn't interested. I went to Ward Street Central School, one of three Central Schools in Oldham.

Marian Hesketh

Keeping warm

When I was four years old, I started school at North Moor School. I went there till I was eleven. I liked art, but didn't like maths. One of the teachers was called Miss Smethurst. She liked to sit on the hot water pipes.

Jim Hesketh

Seeing the King and Queen

In 1937, after their coronation, King George VI and Queen Elizabeth visited Oldham. All the children were marched from their various schools to see them. We all had little Union Jacks and were told to wave them. The school also presented us with a little oblong box with chocolate in it, to mark the coronation. We were also given mugs, blue and white, with the King and Queen's pictures on. I was just five and I was very proud.

Sheila Shipp

'Stars and Stripes Forever'

I started at Werneth School when I was four years old. We had to line up outside in the morning and we would march in. They had a wind-up gramophone and they'd play, of all things, 'Stars and Stripes Forever'. Every Friday morning we could take a toy. There

North Moor School, 1930s. The teacher is Miss Smethurst, who liked to sit on the hot water pipes. The boy with the knitted tie in the back row is Jim Hesketh.

Sheila Parsons (Shipp) with her brother Derek and Rover.

were lots of children from well-off families in the school. One Friday we were ready for going home and I saw this little teddy bear on the floor. I picked it up and I brought it home for my little sister, who had no toys. I was only four. The only toy I remember having was a little wooden fort that somebody gave me. Later my mother asked me to give it to a child in our street who had no toys. I did and the next thing I saw he was smashing it with a hammer!

Derek Lloyd

Baths and biscuits

When I was four, I started at St Peter's School on Union Street. Opposite the school, across Clegg Street, was the Public Baths. Me and my friend Mary used to have a bath there on Saturday mornings, because we had no baths in our houses. We used to cut across behind the library on our way to school; there was a Friends' Sunday School there and the gas works was at the back there. I liked the school. The headmaster was Mr Jones; he lived on Edward Street and he was nice. In the Juniors' the head teacher was Mrs Roper. During the war we had a teacher called Mrs Lyle; she looked positively ancient – her hair was white. She had come back because there was a shortage of teachers during the war. The classes were quite big, between thirty and forty in a mixed class. We had wooden desks for two, with the seats attached and two little inkwells and a place to put your pen. I liked arithmetic but I never liked problems – 'If a train is going this far at this speed...?' They used to worry me silly.

There were two big schoolyards. My uncle Mellor used to come every morning at break time and bring me a biscuit.

Dorothy Knowles

St Peter's School, class 1, in 1936. Children play on the slide.

St Peter's School, Standard 3, 1911. Dorothy Marshall's (Knowles') uncle Billy Mellor is fifth from the right on the front row.

The black book

I went to Higginshaw Infants', Juniors' and Seniors' and left at fifteen; I hated school. The teachers used to have a black book and, if your name got in there two or three times, you would have to go upstairs and they'd get a strap with some tails on and they'd bend you over t'desk and crack you with it. It happened to me twice. If you went home and told your mum and dad, you got another good hiding for getting t'strap. The head teacher at the Senior School was Mr Wannacott.

William Turner

Setting a good example

In the [Clarksfield School] Infants' we used to have a sleep in the afternoon and there were sandpits and things like that to play in. I don't remember much about the Juniors', but I was in the Seniors' during the war and we used to go part-time. We went in the mornings one week, afternoons the next. I think it was because we had disturbed nights because of the air raids. The head of the Juniors' was Mr Pearson and

the Seniors' Mr Watson and I remember Miss Reynolds and Miss Hall. We also had a teacher called Miss Charnock. I liked to do composition. There was another girl who, like me, was good at it. Miss Charnock used to encourage us to do better than each other. When I was in the Seniors', I was a prefect. If children were late or unruly on the stairs going up to class, we used to give them lines – 'I must behave properly on the stairs'. They were supposed to give them to you at the end of the week, but you never got them.

Marian Buckley

A beautiful view?

I went to Beever School, on Beever Street. I believe 'Beever' meant 'Beautiful View'; perhaps it had one when it was built, but not as far as we were concerned. The boys and girls in the school played in different playgrounds. There was a Catholic school next to us, and the boys' playground was on top of our school. So, when it snowed, the boys used to pelt us with snowballs. The headmistress of our school

Clarksfield Infants' School, *c.* 1936. Second row from back, third from left is Marian Hamer (Buckley).

Clarksfield Senior School, *c.* 1945. Third row from back, fourth from left is Marian Hamer (Buckley).

was Miss Winterbottom; my first teacher in the infants' was called Miss Pill; there was also, I think, a Miss Holderness.

The classes were very big. During the war a lot of old teachers came back to teaching, because the young men had joined the forces. The old teachers were very tolerant of us. I liked most things, but I wasn't very good at maths. The teachers used the strap and I had it once; never again. Some of the boys had the strap every day.

Dorothy Bennett

Geography not a strong point

I started school during the war, when I was four. I went to Hathershaw Infants' School. I remember a teacher called Miss McMahon, who had a sister who taught in the Juniors',

just down the yard. There was also a Miss Jones who was very strict and very stern; everyone was frightened of her. When I went to Hollins Secondary Modern the head was Mr Ross. There was Miss Ashworth, Mrs Pilgrim and Miss Casson, and two Mr Taylors, George and John. George Taylor taught Geography and he once said to me, 'You won't find your way around Oldham, so you'll never get out of it!'

Meryl Taylor

Wagging off

I started school when I was only three at St Anne's Royton. It was a nursery school. They had mattresses on the floor and we had to have a sleep in the afternoon. I stayed there until I took my eleven plus but then we moved down

Freehold County Primary, c. 1950. In the back row with the Fair Isle pullover is Jimmy Bancroft, brother of Phyllis Bancroft (Thomson).

south. I remember desks with a lift-up lid, two holes for ink-pots, and pencils and dipping-in pens. I didn't particularly like school. I had a mate called Arthur Buckley and he and I once wagged it off school. The park off Broadway had shelters at that time, which were half underground. We hid in there. We could see everybody looking for us. We got in trouble for that.

Brian Bardsley

Method in my madness

I started school when I was five. Clarksfield School, which had an Infants' and Juniors' department, and I think Seniors' as well, was not far from where I lived. I was a very fussy little girl; everything had to be just right for me. All my clothes had to match. I wore a little beret with a brooch on it and I was taught that the brooch had to go over my right eye. I used to drive the teachers mad apparently. The war was on while I was in the infants' school. We used to have to go into the shelters. The whole school would be in the shelters and I would still be in the cloakroom, putting that brooch straight over my right eye. If I was going to be blown up, that brooch was going to be in the right place. I wasn't daft – yes, I did put that brooch straight – but, if I was last in the shelters, it was because I hated them so, and you are the first person I've ever told that to!

Joyce Mills

Young to be a truant

My first school was Freehold Infants' School. I remember them putting us to bed in the afternoon and I remember being given milk. I hated the bed and the milk. It was often freezing in the mornings and they put the milk near the pipes to thaw it; so it had icy bits in it. I used to play truant from school and even-tually my mother had to take me away. One of the teachers once shoved me in the back and pushed my teeth into the milk bottle; and they made me sit next to a boy with a runny nose. So I played truant. My mum was in our butcher's shop and the school board officer came and said, 'Mrs Bancroft, your daughter is not at school'. 'Oh, yes! I sent her to school!'

Then they went in the back and I was hiding under the table. So mum eventually sent me to Werneth Convent.

Phyllis Thomson

My little mum and Miss Dewsbury

My mum wanted me to take the entrance examination for Hulme Grammar School for Girls. Werneth Convent, for some reason, didn't enter me for the exam, so I missed it. My little mother, brought up with no mum herself, no shoes and very little food, made an appointment to see Miss Dewsbury, the head-mistress of Hulme Grammar School for Girls. She wanted Miss Dewsbury to waive all the rules and let me become a pupil there. Miss Dewsbury said, 'I'm sorry. There are these procedures and your daughter must take the entrance exam if she is to gain admittance'. But she did encourage my brave mum by saying, 'If your daughter has any brains, she will be all right whatever school she goes to'. I went to Counthill.

Phyllis Thomson

Kathleen and John

When I was four and we were living in Derker, I started school at St Anne's in Greenacres. It was a long way to go every day. I had a friend – we still keep in touch – and two big girls held our hands and we went skipping down the yard. Miss Hayden was the headmistress of St Anne's Infants' and Mr Wright was headmaster of the Juniors'. I must have been

Werneth Preparatory School, *c.* 1948. Middle row, extreme left: Phyllis Bancroft (Thomson).

Above: Westwood Infants' School, 1947.

Opposite: Robin Hill Secondary, class 3B, 1956. Back row, third from left: Tom Richmond. The teacher is Hopwood Morgan.

one of those children who told a tale or two because the teacher regularly used to say to me, 'Will you tell the class a story, Kathleen?' There was one teacher called Miss Walsh, who was lovely. She used to tell us a story about a little girl called Kathleen and a little boy called John. I adored her because I thought she was talking about me. When I was twelve I went to St Mary's School at Rhodes Bank. The headmistress was Sister Mary Trace.

Kathleen John

Taking one's whacks

My schooldays began at Westwood Infant/ Junior School on Middleton Road. It was about a mile away from where I lived. It's still there and still a school. The headmaster was Mr Pomeroy and our class teacher was Mrs Broadbent. I remember her as a typical schoolteacher. I stayed there till I was eleven, then I moved to Richmond Secondary School, on Winterbottom Street in Oldham. While I was there we moved from Richmond to Robin Hill, Chadderton Road. I loved Geography and sports at school, but not Maths. The headmaster at secondary school was George Worthington, who had been in the army. He had a strap and I did get strapped. It was a case of, 'Hold your hand out!' and you'd get three whacks. Lads used to pull their hands away, but the teachers had a knack of grabbing your wrist to stop you doing that. The strap hurt, but it was a punishment wasn't it? And you didn't go home and tell your mother.

Tom Richmond

Is his arm tired yet?

I started school at Clarksfield School in 1952. It was an Infant and Junior school. The head of the Juniors was Mr H. Gwyn Thomas; the Infants' headmistress was Mrs Catanach. Miss Taylor taught us in the reception class. I once got strapped because my needlework was poor; I hated needlework. We also got strapped for talking, and I talked a lot. They actually used to line us up to strap us. The art was to get to the end of the line, so the teacher's arm was tired when they got to you. I passed the eleven plus and went to Greenhill Grammar School on Greengate Street where I stayed until I was eighteen.

Isabel Lunn

Blowing a gale

I received part of my early schooling at Strinesdale Open Air School, where I spent three years. It was up on the hills near Oldham, where the tuberculosis sanatorium also was. The whole school was made up of pavilions with huge sliding glass windows. The windows had to remain open all day. In winter you'd sit there wearing a balaclava, the wind whistling though the room. It must have done us good, because after three years I had no health problems at all. After lunch we had an obligatory siesta; we had to lie down on camp beds in the main hall, which we didn't mind, because it was the only part of the building that was heated. The place was very much in the countryside; only part of the playground was flagged over; the rest was grass. We used to roam about playing cowboys and Indians in the long grass. We got a good schooling there. When I returned to Alexandra School, I was put in the second year of the Juniors'. Some people were struggling with their times tables and some had a reading age way behind mine. The headmaster there then was Fred Hundle, not a man of great physical stature, but he had a commanding presence. He ran a tight ship.

When I was in Junior 4 there was one teacher who was too handy with the strap. We lads used to mutter among ourselves and I decided I was going to steal his strap and destroy it. I did so. He mounted a campaign for a couple of weeks to find out who had done it; eventually someone shopped me.

Michael Mills

I didn't do it, honest!

Werneth Convent Preparatory School had very strict rules. One of them, I remember, was that, when pupils were walking along, they had to walk in single file and not block the pavement. In my final summer at the school it acquired a new building. Just before I left some names were discovered on a door-post in the new building, including mine. I protested my innocence vehemently, but sadly no-one believed me.

Phyllis Thomson

four

People and Places

My mum and dad

My mother, Hannah, was a lady, and I mean lady. I don't know where her antecedents were, but she was a very gracious lady. Everybody said it was a joy to come to see her. She wasn't like me. I was always on the front row, always the first child to be up saying a nursery rhyme. No, my mother was a lady. Her father came from Ashton-in-Makerfield and had walked to Oldham because there was no work.

My father's family had come from Morecambe to live in Hollinwood. Dad was a labourer, working outdoors. He got about eighteen shillings a week. At one time he went round with a brass can and sold black peas. His brother, Harry Woodward, was younger and he could sell stale bread to a baker. He ended up with five cars going round with a van at the back, selling peas and pies. But my dad wasn't a success. He was a gentle man. He didn't go to church but he encouraged us to go. He never hit us and I never heard him swear. He and my mother were good people. Years later, when the first man landed on the moon, my granddaughter was playing with her shop. My mother told her to watch the TV, though she

Above: Mrs Hannah Woodward, mother of Mary Timms.

Opposite: Mary Patterson, Wilfred Finnegan's grandma, who swore by cabbage water.

didn't want to. 'You will watch', my mother said, 'this is history. When I was born there was nothing faster than a horse!'

Mary Timms

Cabbage water

My grandmother, Mary Patterson, lived on Cochran Street, near Oldham Edge. We used to go to see her every Sunday, after church. She always boiled cabbage on a Sunday and she never threw the water away. She maintained that the good of the cabbage was in

that water. She'd pour us each a glass of cabbage water, which we had to drink; then we would get a penny. But we had to drink the cabbage water first.

Wilfred Finnegan

No means no

If my mother said you could have something, you could have it. If she said you couldn't, you couldn't. We used to go swimming at Hathershaw Baths. If we were naughty, she'd say, 'Right, you don't go swimming next Tuesday'. Come the next Tuesday and you'd say, 'Can I go swimming?' She'd say, 'What did I tell you?' and you didn't go. And it was worse if you kept asking, because she would say, 'If you keep asking, you won't go next Tuesday either'. So you didn't ask again. My father never raised his hand, but mum did. If we were naughty, we got one on the leg, and we felt it. But she was a good person; she was my mum.

Meryl Taylor

Mrs Hoyle and the mice

In the infants' section at Moorside Village School we had a wonderful teacher. She was called Mrs Hoyle, the same name as me, and was the wife one of my dad's cousins. She had no family of her own, but she was wonderful with children. Every afternoon, about three o'clock, we had to put our heads on our arms on top of the desks, as a sort of relaxation. She would sit there behind her desk and she used to spread breadcrumbs on the floor. We had one of those air gratings. The mice used to come up after the bread, and she would sit there among them. Then, when she thought she had given it enough time, she would stamp her feet, and down the mice would go again.

Ronald Hoyle

The Lancashire Handbag Company

I left school at fourteen and was expected, like all the rest of my family, to get a job in the mill. But there were no vacancies so I went to work at the Lancashire Handbag Company, which was on Sheffield Street. The war had just started and the management of the Lancashire Handbag Company were all Germans. We hated them and they were not fond of us. One day they took all the Germans away; they interned them all. Then things changed. It wasn't a handbag firm any more, but a Royal Navy Stores.

Emily Smith

My wonderful parents

My parents were both deaf. Dad was profoundly deaf; he couldn't hear a thing. He had been born with inadequate hearing and, at that time, medical science was unable to prevent him going completely deaf at the age of twelve. My mother became deaf as the result of a mastoid. Mother was marvellous at lip-reading. If you faced her and talked quite slowly, she could easily make out what you were saying. Dad couldn't lip-read. You had to talk to him with your hands and I became very proficient at sign language. They had both had a basic education and were very competent at reading, writing and mathematics. I was always amazed at how proficient they were at writing letters and working out money in pounds, shillings and pence. My father was a cop packer, an unskilled job, though he maintained it was a difficult job to do. He spent the whole of the thirties unemployed. Because of his deafness, he was last to know of jobs that were going. We had quite a difficult time then. There was very little money at home and we had to be grateful for what we had to eat. Mum did an awful lot of baking and making bread. My sisters, being three years older than I was, were allowed two slices of bread;

I could only have one and a half. That was the reality of making ends meet on a limited income. I couldn't have grown up in a more loving environment though. Mum was always at home and dad was there a lot of the time because there wasn't any work. My father was Arnold and mum was Alice.

Ernest Walker

Grandad Maiden

My grandad was called Arthur Maiden. He worked in the foundry at Platts. His father had died when he was young and he was brought up at the Bluecoat School in Oldham. The boys normally stayed there at weekends, but his mother wouldn't let him stay. He lived with us when he was older. My mother said that nobody could be neater at folding their clothes. When she did the wash, he folded his clothes and put them away. His rooms were always neat. He was fond of different sayings. One night it was quite light but very cold. He used to say, 'As days lengthen, cold strengthens'. In winter he would say, 'February fill dyke, either black or white'. That meant it either rained or snowed.

Winnie Maiden

Courtesy pays

Mum and dad had a butcher's shop in Werneth, Bancroft's Butchers. At the top of Bath Street, where we lived, there was a double-fronted house, where a Mr and Mrs Smith lived. They had the butcher's before my parents. Mr Smith died. Lots of butchers wanted to buy his business, including large ones like Dewhursts. They realised that the shop was in a prime location on the main road. My parents wanted it, but didn't think they stood a chance because they had to raise the money first. Lots of people went to ask about buying the business, but mum and dad didn't go until after

Mrs Lily Shoebridge and neighbour, Mrs Annie Hawkins in the back garden of 98 Schofield Street. The building in the background is the Lancashire Handbag Company.

Mr Arnold Walker and his wife, Alice, 'listening' to their daughter Joyce, who is using sign language.

Mr Smith was buried. When they asked Mrs Smith if she was considering selling, she said that she was, and she would sell to them if they could raise the money. She said she was willing to sell to them because they had had the courtesy to wait until after her husband's funeral before asking; others hadn't.

Phyllis Thompson

Whiteley Street in the 1930s

I lived on Whiteley Street from being born until they demolished all the houses. It was very close to Oldham market. There were two well-known food shops on Oldham market then – Bennett's and Robinson's; they were next door to each other. Robinson's always used to have a big potato pie in the window. You could go in and have your meal there. Sometimes on Saturday afternoons I'd go there washing up, and they'd let me eat the potato pie that was left. At the bottom of Whiteley Street there was a fish and chip shop, three houses, a paper shop, then a big pub – the Postman's Knock – on the corner. Then there was Rope Street, a corner shop, a pawn shop, the Woodman public house, then four big houses with cellars underneath, all owned by market people. Right at the corner was a big billiard hall. As you went up Whiteley Street, on the left hand side, there were big warehouses for storing stuff from the market. Then there was Ross' coal yard, old father Ross. People ordered coal, he weighed it and I often took it to them in a barrow. I think he had some connection with the circus world. Sometimes, on the spare ground at the side of the coal yard, facing where I lived, the circus people put their caravans when the circus came to town.

Stuart McDonough

Joe Hague and his apprentice, James Bancroft, outside Joe's butcher shop.

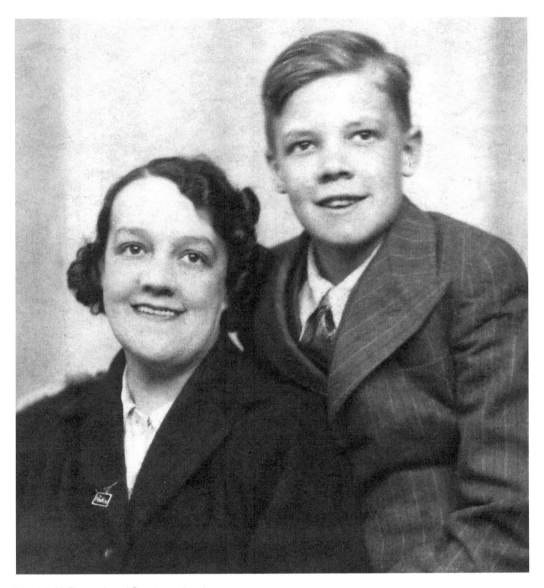

Mrs Ada McDonough and Stuart, aged twelve.

Nelly Knowles, my mother

Belgrave Road, where I lived as a child in the 1930s, is a very long road. We lived on the part that wasn't very posh but the houses on the other part had bay windows – a cut above us. There was an orphanage, the Olive Clayton Orphanage, and all the children went to Hathershaw School. My mother, Nelly Knowles, worked there as a caretaker. She was a very warm character and, on Mother's Day, it was my mother all the children at the orphanage sent cards to. If they lost their dinner money, it was my mother who gave them money to pay for their dinners. Mum was a well-respected and loved woman. If anyone on Belgrave Street had a form to fill in, it was my mother they came to for advice. She had not had a good education; she left school at

Mon(ic)a Proctor, Dorothy Knowles' mum, *c*. 1927.

twelve to work part-time in the mill. But she was very sensible and was always willing to help people. If a lady in the street was having a baby, it was my mother who sat up with her. Everybody knew and loved her.

Marian Hesketh

My father, the character

My father was John Fitzgerald. He was a funny man, the life and soul of any party. He'd go in the pub and all the lads would sit round him and he'd tell them jokes. They loved him. If he had no money, he only had to go in a pub and somebody would buy him a pint. He was a plasterer's labourer, one of the best. He worked for a halfpenny an hour. Then he'd pack the job in and go to work for somebody else. His former employer would say, 'Come back and work for me, and I'll give you a penny an hour'. This went on all through my school life. I remember his boss once shouting me, 'Hey, young Fitz, tell your dad that, if he'll come back and work for me, I'll give him one and a half pence'. That was a lot of money in the late 1930s.

Kathleen John

Single mum in the 1930s

My mother lived in Harpurhey. Her family were staunch Catholics. When she found herself pregnant with my brother, her three sisters were angry. So my grandma put her into the workhouse. When grandad came home, he asked where she was. When he knew, he said, 'There's no daughter of mine going in the workhouse'. He went and fetched her and rented her a room on Retiro Street in Oldham, out of the family's way. She and my dad were never married; he was in the Merchant Navy and she only saw him when he came home on leave. After they became involved she discovered he already had a wife in Sheffield. My brother was brought up by my grandma in Harpurhey. My mum was a hard-working woman. She worked as a cook.

She had quite a hard time, but I was never deprived of anything. I was always well-dressed. There was a furniture shop on Union Street called Billy Weeder's. Mum used to get furniture from him. She'd pay so much a week and she wouldn't get the goods until she had paid the whole amount. She paid out of her wage, whatever she could afford. He was really good with her and would knock quite a bit off the price.

Dorothy Knowles

P.C. Bobby Finney

One day, when I was about eight, I fell out with Jamie Whitehead, one of the boys I used to play with. I had an orange, and I was smearing the juice down a window. Bobby Finney, the policeman, came along. 'Winnie Maiden, ' he said, 'what are you doing?' 'Well, I fell out with Jamie Whitehead'. 'That won't get Jamie Whitehead', he said. 'You are just upsetting his mother'. He took his cloak off and swiped me with it. 'You are not to do that again. I will tell your mother'. And all it was was orange juice down a window!

Winnie Maiden

Respecting policemen

When I was a boy, we respected policeman. We weren't frightened of them. Our parents told us that, if a policeman said, 'Jump', you jumped. And you never argued with a policeman. If you put your foot on the grass in the park, the policeman, Bobby Finney – everybody in Oldham knew Bobby Finney – would smack you with his cane. He didn't hurt you. You didn't dare go home and tell your father, or else you'd get another clout.

Derek Dyson

Wood Park Colliery

When I left school in the 1930s, I wanted to go to work in the colliery. My mother was not happy about it; she wanted me to become apprenticed to one of the trades − joiner, plumber, electrician − but those apprentices were only paid ten shillings a week. As soon as I left school, my mother lost five shillings off her pension; so I would have been working for five shillings a week. A fourteen-year-old boy working in the pit got eighteen shillings a week, a big difference. So I got a job at Wood Park Colliery. At fourteen I was loading coal at the pit bottom into a cage. The cage came down empty from the top of the shaft and we loaded it up. It was hard work, but I enjoyed it. When I started work, they had just opened some pit baths. You had a clean locker for the clothes you went home in and a dirty locker for your pit clothes. In the morning you went to the clean side, undressed, picked your towel and soap up and went to your dirty locker; you put your pit clothes on, filled your water bottle and then went down the pit. After the shift you undressed in the dirty side, went in the showers, came out nice and clean, put your clean clothes on and went home. I worked there for twenty-seven years. The colliery employed about four hundred men. The pit workings were very widespread; sometimes we had to walk three and a half miles to the coalface. Wood Park was owned by the Chamber Colliery Company, who also owned the Oak Colliery at Hollins Road and the Snipe at Ashton, till they were taken over by the National Coal Board. Things were very different when that happened. In the loading bay, where the coal was loaded into wagons, there was always a lot of spillage. A deputy would say to Jack Jones and me, 'Clean it up and I'll give you a quarter'. That meant we got paid a quarter of a shift. It might only take us half an hour, but we still got paid a quarter of a shift. That stopped when the Coal Board took over. I worked from 7.00 a.m. till 3.00 p.m. − 7.00 a.m. till 1.00 p.m. on Saturdays − and came home with seventeen shillings and some pence after I'd paid stoppages.

Wilfred Finnegan

Listening to Milly

Oldham Tommyfield Market was a fascinating place. A relative of mine, who lived in Warrington, loved to come to visit us in Oldham. She would say, 'I must go to Tommyfield'. We would all go to the market and we'd stand there listening to Milly. She used to sell bedding, and she'd shout, 'I don't want five pounds for this; I don't want three pounds. Who'll give me one pound?' People used to stand there five or six deep listening to Milly. 'I've just got five of these. Who wants them?' She always sold them. Listening to Milly was the highlight of my relative's visit.

Meryl Taylor

'A certain dignity'

When I was a child on Belgrave Street, two elderly ladies lived across the way from us, two old maids as people used to call them then. We used to go into their house and they would show us their china. One of them used to lend us books; they were all classics, Dickens and such. When she loaned us a book, the first thing my father did was make us cover it with paper, so it was kept clean. He brought us up with the highest morals and thoughtfulness really. The two ladies were Miss Golding and Miss Birtwhistle. Like all the people in the street, they did not have much money; what they did have was a certain dignity.

Marian Hesketh

Wilfred Finnegan – miner.

The music teacher

When I was eight, my mother started me on piano lessons at the Lyceum. Because I was in a girls' school, she made sure that I went to a male teacher. He was the principal, Leslie Clifton, one of the finest musicians you would ever wish to meet. He recognised me for the bumptious character that I was and he kept his thumb firmly down on me, teaching me humility among other things. After about four years, my mother asked him how I was doing, and he replied, 'Oh, it's early days yet'. He was a super teacher and I had great respect for him. He was organist at St Thomas' Moorside for a long time, and then at Saddleworth church.

Phyllis Thomson

'They're all puddled'

I used to go and visit my grandfather, who lived up Derker in a bungalow. He was called Luke Smith and he lived till he was past ninety. He always used to say to me, 'They're all puddled in this family, only thee and me'. Even up to his dying, when I was married and had children, he always used to give me a penny and an Uncle Joe cough sweet.

Kathleen John

Working for Mr Vickers

On Oak Road, which was perhaps one hundred and fifty yards from where I lived on Hazel Lane as a child, there was a butcher's shop. The manager was Mr Vickers, who eventually came to own the shop. He was a kindly man. He knew that my mother had five children and that money was not in abundance, so when I was eleven he gave me the opportunity to become a butcher's boy. I had to clean the metal bars from which the meat hooks hung and clean the floors, sweeping up the sawdust. I also had to mop the step twice a week. For all that I got the princely sum of ten shillings a week, but paperboys only got seven. I had to make Mr Vickers' tea. He liked sergeant major's tea – two spoonfuls of tea in a genuine pint pot, with four or five spoonfuls of sugar and the top half-inch had to be filled with treated milk. The shop had a big walk-in fridge, six feet by six feet by six feet. It had a big door and inside were all these pieces of meat. It used to terrify me, and Mr Vickers used to say, 'If you don't behave, you'll be locked in'. When I started making meat deliveries on the butcher's bike, I used to take parcels of meat out wrapped in white paper, with an outer wrapping. One day the bike feel over and all the meat fell out. I did my best to sort it out but I didn't know who was getting what. Next day a lady came in the shop and said, 'I was very grateful to you, Mr Vickers, for letting me have a piece of meat, when I was expecting some stewing steak'. 'Oh, did I' he said. He never knew what had happened.

Ernest Walker

Luke Smith (left) with his family.

The folk of Robson Street

When I was a child on Robson Street, everybody knew everybody. They didn't live in each other's pockets, but, if there was trouble, they were there. We had a lady living at the bottom of the road; every Sunday morning she would come out of her house and a cloud of blue smoke would follow her; she'd be cooking her husband's breakfast. Across from us there was a lady who had a daughter who was deaf and dumb. The mother liked a drink and the poor daughter had to cope with her. When she got drunk, they used to hang her on the spikes at St Peter's church. Then somebody would go and tell her daughter and she would have to go and fetch her home. All the kids would be running round them, laughing and jeering. Another lady across the road from us always used to bake my dad a huge muffin when he came home on leave. When she sent me in with it, he used to cringe and say, 'Oh Lord, not another one of them muffins!' At the bottom of Robson Street, on Gas Street, Oldham Corporation had a tip. There were also horses, shire horses, and they used to dress them up. We kids used to go and watch these horses. The Corporation tip stretched from Waterloo Street to Roscoe Street, just before you get to Rhodes Bank. There also used to be a mortuary there. Although Robson Street was right in the centre of Oldham, it was a very nice place to live.

Dorothy Knowles

Mixing with royalty

My husband was Lord Mayor of Oldham and I very much enjoyed being Lady Mayoress. We met Princess Anne, when she came to open a new part of the hospice. She was very nice, very straight. We also met Princess Margaret and Princess Diana. We were invited

Dorothy and Norman Bennett's wedding in 1954. Norman became Lord Mayor of Oldham and Dorothy Lady Mayoress.

to Manchester Airport for the opening of the second terminal. That was a fantastic day. The Queen should have opened it, but she was poorly, so the Duke of Edinburgh stood in for her. We met the Queen at the garden party here in Oldham and again at a garden party at Buckingham Palace. The Queen visited Alexandra Park in Oldham and when she arrived, she got out of the car and said, 'What a beautiful park you have!'

Dorothy Bennett

Cold feet

In 1938 I was due to get married at St Margaret's church, Hollinwood. I'd got every-

Charles Frederick Lord (with flat cap) who would have killed Lillian's wavering fiancé.

thing for the wedding and had been down Manchester for my wedding dress. My fiancé was living with his mother; he was supposed to be ill in bed with flu.

I got a message that he wanted to see me because he had something to tell me. He said he'd changed his mind, he didn't want to get married. I said I was going home to tell my father, who would have killed him. He followed me and said he didn't mean it. We were married, but we should never have been. My children were the only good thing that came out of my marriage. He left me when the oldest was five. He went out of the door, waved and said, 'See you' and disappeared from our lives. I did see him again, always with another woman, and I gave him a good kicking.

Lillian Wood

Send for the Pied Piper

When I was a little girl, we lived in a very old house. My mum had a big mug. There was a rat on the stairs and my dad threw the mug at it and broke the mug. Mum and Dad had lived right in the centre of Oldham, near where the market was. She once told me that at twelve o'clock at night the place was full of rats, running down the streets. Nobody used to go out that late at night. When we moved to a council house, we couldn't afford wallpaper; so we had distemper on the walls. The people who could afford paper had bugs, because they used to make the wallpaper paste out of flour and water, which attracted bugs. We were the only ones who didn't have bugs, because there was lime in the distemper and my dad used to lime wash the ceilings. The lime kept the bugs away. There was something to be said for being poor.

Kathleen John

five

The Wonderful World of Work

Joy turned to ashes

I left school in 1946, when I was fourteen and I got my first job, sewing. When I had finished my first week's work. I went home and proudly gave my mum my first wage, all of fifteen shillings. It was a ten shilling note and five shillings in coins. Mum put the money on the left-hand side of the fireplace, which was where she usually popped things until we had had our meal. After the meal she said it was time to start cleaning; it was Thursday and we always cleaned on Thursday. Mum picked up the papers from the side of the fireplace and threw them into the fire, forgetting that my wage was with them. We managed to rescue the coins, though they were badly discoloured. The 10/- note, though, had gone up in flames. All that was left was the ashes. We were, needless to say, both very unhappy.

Dorothy Knowles

Meet Spider-Man

I worked as a steel erector in the thirties. I started on steel work at Woolworths in Oldham. Then we worked on the Grand

Dorothy Marshall (Knowles) second from right. Her workmates are (from left) Gertrude Holt, Joyce Duffy and May Gartside.

The Grand Theatre which became the Gaumont cinema.

Theatre in Union Street. They were converting it to the Gaumont cinema. We put the circle in for the showing of films. I had a bad fall there and ended up in hospital with a spine injury. I went through the roof as well, and fell on the steel works. I was accident prone, certainly not Spider-Man.

Ralph Turner

Post girl at Platt's

When I left school in 1935 I got a job at Platt's, which was a big textile firm. It was at Werneth, on the way to Manchester, on Featherstall Road. They sent engineers to India and all over the world. I can remember being sent to Liverpool to collect passports for fitters who were going abroad the following day. I started as a post girl and went all over the works. It wasn't just one building; there were many buildings, including a sawmill. One day I had to take a cheque to one of the directors for signing. I had to cross over a railway bridge – that's how big the place was – and I was running. A policeman, Bobby King, stopped me. 'Who are you?' 'Winnie Maiden'. 'Who do you work for and where are you going?' 'I work for Mr Clinch and I won't tell you where I'm going. It's confidential'. 'Then you'll come back with me', he says. 'But he is in a hurry; he wants this cheque'. He made me go all the way back with him and I can see Mr Clinch's and Nellie Brown's faces now when I walked in with this policeman. Mr Clinch sorted it all out. While I was working there, King George VI died. One of the workmen popped into the office and said to Nellie Brown, 'King's dead'. 'Well', she said, 'I saw him last night, going up West Street on his bike'. She thought he was talking about Bobby King.

Winnie Maiden

A flock of mothers

I started work, when I left school at fourteen, in an engineering works. At that time my mother, my sister and I were living with my grandad and grandma and an uncle in a house which had two rooms downstairs – a small living room and a kitchen – two little bedrooms, no back door and no hot water. I was four feet two inches and weighed five and a half stone. I had to wear short trousers to work. I went to the canteen at lunchtime with my little box with potato pie, which my grandma had made for me. All the women were going, 'Oh, what are you doing here? Why aren't you in school?' But they all looked after me for years.

Derek Lloyd

The making of a butcher

In the 1920s my first job was in my uncle's butcher's shop on Huddersfield Road. It was Whitehurst's butcher's shop and he was a favourite uncle of mine. While I'd been at school I used to go to the shop at weekends. When I went there to work, the first job on Monday morning was to go to a place called Grains Bar to a farm to collect cattle. In those days there was no transport for the cattle; we had to drive them through the streets to the slaughtering. When a lamb had to be slaughtered, it had to be put on a cradle and a knife stuck in its throat. The first lamb I was told to slaughter wriggled free on me. Herbert, my mate in the slaughterhouse, said, 'Now you can go and catch it!' I didn't mind saving life, but taking life was different. However, by the time I caught that lamb, I could have killed it ten times over. I worked for my uncle for two years, for six shillings a week. Then his son left school and, because work was scarce and he couldn't get a job, he joined his dad in the shop and I had to leave. I worked for a time for a man named John Paton, a big, strong Scottish bloke. He made potted meat and meat paste and things like that in a place on Neild Street, off Copster Hill Road. Eventually my mum and dad bought some property, a shop and living accommodation, at the bottom of Wellington Road. It cost £450 and I took out a twenty year mortgage and paid it back in ten. There were no fridges then; we had an ice box. Eventually, after the traveller kept pestering me, I bought a one hundred cubic feet refrigerator. The shop was fitted by Johnny Woodcock, who lived in Glodwick. The fitting – rails for hanging the meat, counters, knives, hooks – cost £45. Every Saturday morning at noon Johnny Woodcock came round the corner to my shop and I gave him a one pound note, until my debt was paid. The shop was called Hoyle's Butchers and right across the road was Chamber Mill.

Ronald Hoyle

Creelers, cross-ballers and beamers

I left school at Easter 1946 and started work at Lees and Wrigley's cotton mill, off Glodwick Road. You had to work your way up. You began as a creeler, then went as a cross-baller and finally became a beamer. The creelers helped the cross-ballers and the beamers to change the bobbins. When you had been there a little while they used to put you on the cross-ball machine and then on the beamer. I worked there for ten years, until they closed. When I started, I worked from 7.30 a.m. to 5.30 p.m., with one hour for lunch, which my mother made for me at home, because I didn't live far from the mill. On Saturdays we worked 7.30 a.m. to noon. I can't remember my wage when I started, but when I finished at Lees and Wrigley's, in 1956, I was earning £5 a week.

Marian Buckley

A group of cop packers at the Owl Mill in the 1950s.

The ins ... and outs of work

After I left school I started work at a place called Armature Winding, but was only there for a few weeks. Then I went to work in an office for a man called Archie Brown. He had market stalls, but then he started to open shops and wanted somebody to work in his office. I was going to night school for shorthand, but, strangely, not for typing. I applied for the job, as did a number of other people. When they learned who the accountant was, they all dropped out. I did a test and Archie Brown gave me the job. The accountant didn't like it. When he saw me talking to some lads in the warehouse – I was, after all, only a teenager – he sacked me. I next became a roller-coverer at the Hawk Mill, in Shaw. I had to go and see the man who was the main roller-coverer. His nephew, Eddie, happened to be there. I got the job and, over time, because the roller-coverer and as his wife had no children, they used to invite me to tea on Sundays. Their Eddie would be there and we did not get on – he

was a terrible tormentor. One day I said to him, 'I hope I never see you again, as long as I live'. Two years later I married him!

Lily Radcliffe

'Will you take the blame?'

I was always in trouble at school. I remember once turning some water on and wetting a teacher called Miss Brisby all through. I wasn't clever but I wasn't behind the door either. I started work as a weaver in a mill. I wasn't much good at it and made many mistakes. There was a fellow working there that I liked and I used to say to him, 'They'll sack me. Will you take the blame?' The cotton mill I started in was on Manchester Street. A friend of mine, Dora Coppin, worked with me. One day we were acting daft on the stairs and I got sacked, but she didn't. When I see her now, I always say to her, 'It were through you I got sacked'.

Lillian Wood

Apprenticeships

When I left school, I got an apprenticeship at Mather and Platt's after a very strict interview. I was put into the notorious No. 2 Bay, which was staffed by semi-skilled workers and I had to set up and work a capstan lathe. It was jolly hard work, but I made lots of bonus money. We had to attend school two and a half days and three nights a week and were taught by Tommy Davies, the head of Mather and Platt's training school. I understand that he was a sports reporter and wrote articles for the *Manchester Guardian*. Eventually I asked to be transferred to another department, because my friends in other departments were working with skilled men and doing interesting and difficult work and I had learned all I could in No. 2 Bay. The men in charge of the apprentices would not move me. I heard that AVRO, a similar distance from home, required apprentices. Off my own bat I got an interview at AVRO and was accepted. I went on Monday lunchtime to hand my notice in, so that I could leave on Friday. There was a dreadful row. I made more bonus than anyone. I got my week's wages, around one pound, and then I made two or three pence bonus. I remember we used to have to collect our money in a pewter box. I was given a good telling-off, but they let me leave and I never regretted it. I went in the drawing office at AVRO and had to draw packing crates. These were used to send spare parts of aircraft – a wing perhaps, or an aerilon or a rudder – to different parts of the world. The crates I designed were for the Hanson; I don't remember doing anything for the Lancaster or the Shackleton bomber. The crates could be twenty or thirty feet long by two feet high, or as small as three feet by two feet. I worked 8.30 a.m. to 5.00 p.m. and my wage was £1 5s a week.

Ernest Walker

The office junior

When I was fifteen, I started work at the Knoll Spinning Company on Chew Valley Road in Greenfield. I worked there for a few years in the office. I was the office junior and I had to make the boss a cup of tea and take it in to him on a tray. I also had to take over the phones if the telephonist was away. My working hours were 9.00 a.m. to 5.00 p.m., with an hour for lunch. My first pay was just over £2 a week, a lot of money in those days. I used to catch the No. 225 express bus on Copster Hill Road and I either caught that to come home or I got the train that ran from Diggle to Oldham; they called that train the Delph Donkey and I used to get off at Clegg Street station.

Meryl Taylor

Apprentice confectioner

After I left school I got a job at a confectioner's called Beilby's. I served my time there for seven years as an apprentice. It was hard work, but I enjoyed it. The wages were terrible, fifteen shillings for a forty-hour week. I didn't make the bread. A lady called Mildred, who was much older than me, used to start earlier than I did, and she mixed the bread. By the time I got to work she was mixing muffins and teacakes and things like that. We used to wait for them rising and, while that was happening, we used to make scones and what we called club cake; that was a plain scone mix, where you rolled one piece out, put jam on it and put another piece on top; when it was cooked, you put icing sugar on it. We had to tin the bread and the muffins and things like that; then they had to go in the proofers, waiting for them to rise again. Breadmaking is a long process. We used to have workmen on their way to work coming into the shop at 6.30 a.m., earlier on Saturdays. We made all sorts of cream cakes and things like that. People used to say to

Christmas at the AVRO drawing office, *c*. 1955.

Drawing office staff at AVRO. Ernest Walker is second from the right.

me, 'When you have worked here a while, you'll stop eating cakes'. I never did and I still enjoy them. Making wedding cakes and birthday cakes was a part of the job I liked very much. When it came to Christmas and Easter, I used to work all night. We would work all day, have a short break at teatime and then work all night. Then we would work all the next day. I was too tired to get ready to go out to a dance on Christmas Eve. I went to college to learn about baking. It was Oldham Technical College, which was on Ashcroft Street. Beilby's Confectioner was quite a busy shop. Mildred, who worked there with me, was a maiden lady and very nice. There were also two girls called Amy

and Florence who worked in the shop with me.

Dorothy Bennett

Card room girl

From school I started work in a cotton mill, Kirkham and Mannock's, on Green Street. You had to go on whatever was available when you started and I went in the card room. My first month was spent learning and my wage was £2 15s a week. When I had learned the job and had a set of twenty-four cards of my own, my wage went up to £3 10s a week. I worked 7.30 a.m. to 5.30 p.m. with an hour for dinner. I used to give all

Carding.

Four girls from Kirkham and Mannock's. From left to right: Joyce Cooper, Eileen Booth, Mary Smith, Elsie Topping (Turner). They wear headscarves to hide their curlers.

my wage to my mum on a Thursday and I got the odd money back. On Thursdays my friend and I used to climb up to Sunny Farm to see my grandma, and we used to get a quarter of toffees and a bottle of pop from the shop, because we had just been paid.

Elsie Turner

Adding it up

My first job after leaving school was in a garage in Shaw. I used to babysit for the man who owned the garage. I didn't really know what I was doing and I learned the job as I went along. One of my tasks was to deduct from the stocks the petrol that people bought at the garage. One day there was no petrol in the storage tanks. The boss' brother, who ran the place, really laid into me, saying

that I couldn't have been knocking off the total the amounts that people bought. He used a few choice words, which I never heard elsewhere. When I told my father, he went round to see him, and told him, 'She won't be coming back. She'll hear that kind of language soon enough'. When the truth came out, the garage had been burgled and the villains had siphoned all the petrol off.

Marian Hesketh

A start in the cotton mill

I left school at fifteen and went to work in the cotton mill, in the card room, where my mother worked. I was just labouring, fetching and carrying for the cotton machines. I worked forty-five hours a week for £6 15s a week. I wanted to be a stripper and

Above: Mill workers leaving Hartford Mill at the end of their shift. Joyce Walker is on the right at the front. Note the entrance to the air-raid shelter on the left.

Opposite: A group of 'gaffers' at James Stott's Werneth Mill in the 1920s.

grinder, but you couldn't do that until you were eighteen. So I made up my mind to learn all I could about the cotton industry. When I turned eighteen, I went and asked to be allowed to become a stripper and grinder, but they kept putting me off. When my stepfather told me that they wanted an apprentice where he worked, I applied. I was accepted and they started me as a stripper and grinder.

Tom Richmond

'A different life'

I left school at fourteen, when the war was still being fought. There was a store in Oldham, at Mumps Bridge, called Buckley and Prockter. It was like Kendal's in Manchester. The store consisted of several buildings, including, so I was told, one where the assistants originally used to live. I went for an interview and I was given a job. I remember the manageress telling me I was a very lucky girl. She said that their staff had only just stopped having to pay to work there; they did that because they were so well trained that they could go anywhere to work afterwards. I worked in the department where they sold clothes but the assistants had to do some time in every department so that they could answer any questions they might be asked. I worked from 8.45 a.m. till 7.00 p.m. and on Saturdays until 6.00 p.m. I earned 7s 6d a week. The store was patronised by a lot of very rich people. Oldham had a lot of mills then, and the mill owners were very wealthy. Customers would often give you tips, perhaps as much as half a crown (2s 6d). It was a dif-

Left: Buckley and Prockter advertisement.

Opposite: Interior of Buckley and Prockter *c 1912*

Below: Watching a parade outside Buckley and Prockter's.

ferent life. Customers used to come in and, if they wanted to pack something up at home, they would ask if we had any empty boxes. Then they would ask if our van driver could deliver the empty boxes. The atmosphere in the shop was very quiet. We were trained to speak in whispers and never to raise our voices.

Ella Lloyd

The terrible Mr Harris

When I worked at Platt's, I went to night school to learn shorthand and typing. I was assigned to work for a man called Mr Harris. One day I was called in to see him. 'Where have you been till now? I've rung twice for you'. I had been to the ladies' room, but I didn't dare tell him. His secretary, Betty, was in the room and I didn't know what to say. He said, 'Here, then' and he pushed across his desk a basket piled high with letters which fell on the floor. 'You can pick them up,' he said, 'Now get out'. I was terrified of losing my job and when I got back to my desk, I thought I was in serious trouble. Betty came to me and said, 'Why on earth didn't you tell him where you had been?' 'I couldn't', I said. 'I'd been to the ladies' room'. 'Oh', she said, 'I'll make it right'. When I asked her what he had said, she told me Mr Harris had laughed his head off. It didn't make me like him any better!

Winnie Maiden

A nice wedding present

When I left school, I went to work at a mill in Moss Lane, Shaw, over the fields from Derker. I earned £2 a week for the first six weeks and then £4 1s 6d a week. When I was going to be married, my fiancé was a labourer at a place where they made soap powder and we worked up to dinnertime on the day we got married. When he went in to work on the Monday,

Mill girls line up at pay-office to collect their wages.

he was told he was no longer required – a bit rough for a newly married man. He was a Cardiff lad and didn't know much about Oldham. I was working in the mill all day, so my mother took him around looking for a job. He taught himself to be a plasterer and, at the finish, he had his own firm. I was a card-tenter in the card room. I worked at that for years; then I became a box-tenter. It was very hard and dirty work.

Kathleen John

six

Two World Wars

Seeing the funny side

My dad was in the First World War and he got his jaw shot away in France. They were in the trenches and the man next to him had his nose shot off and dad's jaw went. He'd only one or two teeth when he died. The dentists and doctors in the army did very well for him. It was winter and it was snowing. They sent a walking man with them out of the trenches. Dad was holding his jaw, the other man was holding his nose – what was left of it. They went over the fields to this hut, where the First Aid men were. The First Aid man was asleep. The walking man woke him. He took one look at my dad and the other wounded man and he fainted. They had to bring him round before he could attend to them. They brought my dad home to a hospital in Liverpool. First morning an orderly came with dad's breakfast. He looked at dad and said, 'This isn't much good to you, is it mate?'

Thomas Maiden, Winnie Maiden's dad, before he was wounded in the First World War.

Dad could only drink out of a feeding cup; they had sent him a kipper!

Winnie Maiden

A question of sensitivity

Before the First World War dad had worked for the Co-op. He became a manager at Morris Street. A manager's job came up at the Liverpool Emporium, a huge Co-op store. Dad decided he was going to apply for it; it was a much better position, with more money and he knew that he had all the qualifications they wanted. He applied and was called for interview. After the interviews dad was called in and the chairman spoke. 'You've got the best qualifications of any man that we've got, Maiden', he said. 'But what about that face of yours; it won't look right on the shop floor'. Dad explained that his jaw had been shot away in the war but they wouldn't give him the job. My mother told me he came home and said he would never apply for a job again. I remember her saying, 'I will never forgive that man. To tell your dad he'd everything they wanted but his appearance. Why didn't they just say he hadn't got the job?'

Winnie Maiden

Consequences of war

I was four years old when the Great War started. My father fought in it. I can't remember what happened to him while he was in the forces, but when he came back, he was a changed man. All he did after he came home from the war was get drunk. he was never again much use to us as a family.

Ralph Turner

Down with the Kaiser!

I was born in 1914 and was four years old when the Great War ended. My earliest visual

OLDHAM EVENING CHRONICLE, Monday, September 23, 1946.

PRESENTATION TO RETIRING CO-OP EMPLOYEES
Their Years Of Service Total 207

Left to right: Mr. Hutchinson (President of the Board of Management), Mr. Boyd (Boot Manager), Mr. Holroyd (Deputy General Manager), Mr. Ellis (General Manager), Mr. Maiden (Drapery Manager) and Mr. Larder (Secretary).

Affectionate words of farewell were spoken on Saturday at a gathering at the Hill Stores, when four members of the Oldham Equitable Society's staff, Mr. Ernest Ellis (general manager), Mr. Herbert Larder (secretary), Mr. James Boyd (boot manager), and Mr. Thomas Maiden (drapery manager), attended a presentation dinner held in their honour. The four men were retiring after long periods of service with the society. Mr. Ellis has 51 years, Mr. Larder 54, Mr. Maiden 52, and Mr. Boyd 50.

Several speakers paid tributes to the four men, and Mr. H. Holroyd, the deputy general manager, concluded his speech with the words: "Well done, thou good and faithful servants." The whole company drank a toast in honour of the retiring men.

Mr. Ernest Ellis, responding, said it had been a pleasure, privilege and honour to serve.

After the dinner, entertainment was provided by Mr. Wally Benson (pianist) and Mr. Ernest Blackwell (entertainer).

Above: So much for Liverpool Emporium. Thomas Maiden (second from right) retiring after fifty-two years' service with Oldham Co-op.

Right: Annie Maiden, a nurse in the First World War.

Edward and Lily Radcliffe at their wedding in 1943 during the Second World War.

memory is of a harvest display in 1918. A tram came up through Moorside village and all the operatives came out of the mills, clapping and cheering. The tram had a kind of statue on the front, an image of the Kaiser, all tied up with rope.

Ronald Hoyle

Outbreak of war

I was eleven when the war started. A chappie over in Chadderton had started a boys' club in his house. Each summer he used to organise a holiday. In 1939 we were going to Cawsand, a little village the other side of Plymouth Hoe. We went down to Plymouth on the train, then across on a boat. It was very exciting; there were aeroplanes knocking about and barrage balloons. We were coming back on the train on the Sunday after the holiday when news went round that war had broken out. I can remember coming back across the fields from the club one night when the bombs were falling on Manchester.

Jack Halliwell

Appendicitis and air raids

I was seventeen when the war started and I joined the WVS. If there were an air raid, I would go on duty at the Town Hall. I remember vividly the first time the air-raid sirens went in Oldham. I'd been ill the night before; the doctor diagnosed appendicitis and I was rushed into hospital. I was operated on that night, the night the first air-raid warning went in Oldham. The rest of the patients were moved downstairs because of the air-raid warning. I was too ill to move, so I was left on the ward, with a young South African nurse to look after me.

Lily Radcliffe

Mr Sylvester Hamer (Marian Buckley's dad) who served on the ambulances in the First World War.

Air-raid precautions

I was seven years old when the war began. I can remember the blitz in Manchester. Me and my mum and dad were coming up Cranbrook Street and the sky over Manchester was lit up with the fires. I can also remember the people, on Christmas Day, streaming up Brewerton Street to see what had happened when the doodlebug fell on Abbey Hills. When the sirens went in the night we would come downstairs and my dad would put two boxes, like orange boxes, and an ironing board together and I would sleep in there. Or we used to sit in the pantry, because they used to say that

Lily Radcliffe in the living room of 2 Butterworth Street in 1943. Note the radio and the blackleaded fireplace and oven.

was the safest place. With all the tinned stuff on the shelves we would have got knocked out!

Marian Buckley

Jars of sweets

I was nearly eight when the war started. I remember we were in lines in the school yard; we had our arms about each other and we were marching around the yard chanting 'We want war; we want war', the way kids would. We used to have shelter practice every Friday afternoon. The boys would be given jars of sweets to carry down into the shelters. We never got them and I often wonder what happened to those sweets. They would certainly have passed their sell-by date by now!

Dorothy Bennett

Wartime memories

I can remember the air raids. When the sirens went my mother used to collect us and we walked to the top of our street to the air-raid shelter which was under St Patrick's School. It was a club really, with snooker tables in, but during the war they used it as an air-raid shelter. You might be in the shelter all night, but next morning people still had to go to work and kids to school. My sister was an air-raid warden, my dad was on street patrol. I always remember them putting their steel helmets on; then off they'd go, patrolling the streets. There were soldiers stationed in Alexandra Park. Up on West Street there was a barrage balloon; it was moored there. I remember doing the shopping for my mother with the ration books. If the greengrocer got some fruit in, you had to run and join the queue. I spent hours and hours standing in the queue

Ann Wood and her brother David. Ann was born during an air raid.

Above and below: Two photographs of bomb damage after an air raid in 1941.

at greengrocer's and confectioner's. I can remember identity cards.

Derek Dyson

One way to empty a hospital

In summer 1939 I was in hospital in Oldham, expecting my second child. The authorities expected that Hitler would bomb Britain straight away and Oldham hospital was designated to receive Manchester casualties. So they emptied the hospital, sent everybody home. The road by the hospital and Latics football ground was full of cars and buses with their windows dolly blue. You didn't take your own clothes into hospital then; you wore a nightgown with a white flannel bed-jacket. Also you only got your dinner. Relatives could bring food in for you. I had written to my mother, asking her to bring me some cream crackers and some apricot jam – a rare treat. My mother was sitting at the door of her house in Hollinwood, reading my letter, when a car pulled up. To her astonishment there was I, in my nightie. They had sent us all home. It was a wonder we didn't have our babies there and then!

Mary Timms

Bombs and babies

My daughter was born during the Second World War. I had started in labour and I had to be rushed into Boundary Park Hospital. There was an air raid going on and bombs were dropping. The hospital had trouble contacting my doctor and my baby was coming fast. He eventually arrived and my daughter was born. I was covered with blood and they had to move me to another room. While I was having my baby the bed was shaking with the noise of all the bombs dropping.

Lillian Wood

Nearer my God to thee

In 1941 I was eight years old and we were living on Fourth Avenue. When Manchester was blitzed, all the tiles on our house were blown off. Many windows were blown out. Bombs fell on Hollinwood cemetery, which was only 200 yards away. We were evacuated to the Salvation Army citadel in Hollinwood, near to the Roxy cinema. We stayed there for several weeks, while the house was being repaired. We slept on mattresses which they laid on the floor. I think they had to be moved in the mornings so that tables could be set up for us to have breakfast.

Ernest Walker

You must come home!

I was a teenager during the war years. Like all teenagers, I liked to go out, to the pictures, dancing, etc. My mum gave me strict instructions. 'If the sirens sound, you must come home straightaway, no matter where you are'. So I could be halfway through a film, I could be at a dance – if the sirens sounded, I had to go home. My mother was afraid, I knew that, but, being a teenager, I didn't see it that way. I remember sitting in the cinema and a notice came up on the screen, THE SIRENS HAVE JUST SOUNDED. ANYONE WISHING TO LEAVE THE CINEMA PLEASE DO SO. I had to get up and go. I would run across Union Street, in the blackout, with the sirens sounding and the ack-ack going as the guns tried to shoot the planes out of the sky.

Emily Smith

Devastation on Abbey Hills Road

It was Christmas Eve, 1944. I'd been to the Odeon. We were all in bed. An evacuee called Alan, from Walthamstow, was living with us then and we had a little dog, called Kiltie. In the middle of the night we heard such a crash.

Above: Winnie Maiden with Kiltie in Abbey Hills.

Left: Alan, the evacuee, with Kiltie.

I said, 'Oh, they've brought him down', thinking it was an aircraft; but it was a doodlebug. We got up. It was pitch black because you couldn't put a light on. I told Alan to get up and get dressed as best he could. We could hear little Kiltie scratching at the door downstairs. Mother just beat me downstairs and she said, 'What were you doing last night? You've left the door open'. Of course it was the doodlebug exploding that had burst the door open; amazingly all the glass was intact, though the glass in all the other rooms was smashed. I had heard mother and father arguing a few minutes before. 'Aren't things bad enough without you two falling out?' I said. Father told me that, as he got in bed, he had put his clothes on the chair by the bed. The blast had picked the chair up and flung it across the room, so he couldn't find his trousers. I couldn't stop laughing. We looked round the house as best we could. Everywhere was soot and glass. The roof had held though. We went out onto the street to see what we could do and realised the full horror of what had happened. Paul Travis had lost two children. Mr and Mrs Bowker had two children, one nine, one eleven. Mr Bowker had gone on duty when the siren sounded. The two children were sleeping either side of Mrs Bowker and the blast had taken them both. My father worked for the Co-op; he managed the drapery, but, because they had no funeral department then, he dealt with the funerals. He said, 'Winnie, I think some of these poor people will be coming to see me in the morning. Try to get one of the rooms ready; clear up the soot and glass'. I remember that Mr Bowker came to make the arrangements and they took the bodies in St Mark's church. It was Christmas Day and my cousins were coming by train – trains ran on Christmas Day then – from Wigan to spend the day with us. Of course we had no phone and they had no phone. They had set out and they got off the train at Clegg Street station and were walking up Waterloo Street. My uncle said, 'Someone's been celebrating. That shop window's gone' Of course it was the blast. There was nothing but fields either side of Abbey Hills Road and the doodlebug came down on the houses.

Winnie Maiden

A child's wartime memories

I was only two when the war started. My sister and I lived with our parents on Schofield Street, Hathershaw. We had an Anderson shelter in our garden and my father put a little stove in and some small cans of soup, so that if we had to go in the shelter during the night we would have something warm to eat. The man next door had a shelter which he had dug out of his lawn. He dug down and used sandbags and his family went in there. I can remember going in the Anderson shelter on Christmas Eve 1944 when the bomb fell on Abbey Hills. I can still see the flash now and we had a lot of shrapnel in our garden. Sometimes we were in the shelter for half an hour, sometimes for hours. The Lancashire Handbag Company was across the road from our house. The air-raid siren was on there. When the siren went off, it shook the house. My father was on the fire alert service. The fire service was based at Hemingway's garage on Hollins Road. They used to stay there during the night.

Meryl Taylor

Keeping safe

Our house had a cellar and during the war, if the sirens went, we used to go down there. There was room for a camp bed. Sometimes I would be asleep; my mum would bring me down and take me back again after the all clear, and I knew nothing about it. The houses where we lived had a big communal back, and

16th Royal Engineers, 167th Bomb Disposal Squad. Middle row, extreme right: Thomas McTighe, Mary Timms' first husband.

16th Royal Engineers, 167th Bomb Disposal Squad with a 1,000lb bomb.

there was an air-raid shelter in there for the houses. I seem to remember that one time a bomb fell near Oldham Athletic football ground. It was resting on the clothes-lines and they had to evacuate all the houses.

Brian Bardsley

Courage and kindness

My husband was called up and put in the bomb disposal squad. He was stationed in Cardiff. There were thirty-two men in the squad and they lived in a big house. I went down to Cardiff to see him and I met the other members of the squad and got to know them a little. My son was just three and I took him with me. We had a nice time there – our first holiday. My husband came to see us off on Cardiff station. While we were there waiting for the train, a porter came along with a coffin. My husband said, 'It'll be some soldier that's got killed. They'll be sending him home'. That was the last time I saw him. A fortnight later they were sending him home. Normally you never find out how a soldier died, but my mother-in-law said to me, when I got the telegram telling me of his death, 'Why don't you go down to Cardiff and see what happened?' So I did. I took my sister-in-law with me. The train was absolutely packed and it was midnight when it got to Cardiff. Two people got off the train, who had a taxi waiting to take them to Llandaff. We were going to Whitchurch, which is the other side of Cardiff. They insisted on taking me to the house where my son and I had stayed a couple of weeks earlier. We had to knock the lady up, but she took us in, gave us a bed and never charged us for it. Next morning I went to the house where the bomb disposal lads were. While I was waiting to see the officer, they were telling me what had happened. They were laying mines; there was an explosion and they were all thrown the length of a football

field. Their officer came, only a young man, and he conducted a roll call. Of course, Mike, as they called my husband, did not answer his name. The officer, who had just won the George Cross for diving into a tank of oil and removing a detonator, told them to go back to work. When they wouldn't, he took out his gun and said, 'If you don't go back to work, I'll shoot you'. The officer himself said to me, 'There was I, my first big job. He was the first lad I'd lost. I had to stand there and pretend that I couldn't care less, when all I wanted to do was run like hell away from that minefield'. They were kindness itself to me. When the coffin came home, I knew that it was filled with sand. I think all they found of my husband was a piece of his elbow.

Mary Timms

Smelling fear

I had two elderly aunts, who lived in Uxbridge. When the flying bombs started, they asked if they could come and stay with us. I had never felt frightened, but, because they were frightened, so was I. Underneath the stairs in our house there was a little pantry. When the sirens went, I would be shoved into this pantry and the two aunts came in after me. I used to watch the flying bombs heading for Liverpool. That Christmas Eve in 1944 we saw one, and one of my aunts said, 'That bomb's not going to Liverpool; it's coming here'. And it was; it fell on Glodwick. My parents pushed me into the pantry with the two aunts and that day I not only felt fear, I smelled it.

Joyce Mills

Collecting shrapnel

During the war they moored barrage balloons on Oldham market. They also brought a Spitfire, already assembled, for the public to look at. There were three men to guard it.

Sometimes we would see the sky red from the fires in Manchester after an air raid. We would hear the shrapnel dropping on the roofs. There would be a lot of it and next day we'd go round collecting pieces of shrapnel.

Stuart McDonough

Over the rainbow

My only memory of the war is of going into the shelter at school. We all had to go in there. I used to stand up and sing that Judy Garland song 'Over the Rainbow'. I don't know why, because I can't sing for toffee. My dad worked on building the air-raid shelters and he had a fall and broke something. I remember coming home and making chips for his dinner. I went back to school and we did our daily news. I wrote that I had been making chips and teacher said, 'Aren't you a bit young to be making chips?' I was about five or six at the time.

Kathleen John

Rose Queens and evacuees

Every year the Oldham Parish Church would choose a Rose Queen, who used to walk with her court in procession. The year that I was chosen the war had started, with clothing coupons and rationing. So they couldn't have a Rose Queen. They decided instead to have a big campaign in Oldham collecting salvage. I was chosen, with helpers, to go round in our area, collecting newspapers for the war effort. I was just seven. We had a boy from Guernsey as an evacuee. Leonard came to us in 1942 and he stayed until just after the war. My mother used to be in a group which met on Wednesday evenings. I used to go with her and we met in one of the group's houses. We would knit little squares to make blankets for the men in the forces. We used any oddments of wool that we could get and then someone

had the job of stitching the squares together. We also made gloves, scarves and balaclavas.

Sheila Shipp

The hysterical lady

I was seven when the war started and thirteen when it finished. When the sirens went, we used to go down to the Corporation site at the bottom of Robson Street. We used to go into the shelter underneath the site. The Corporation kept shire horses there and we could hear their hooves clattering above our heads when they got excited. The Corporation had put benches in there for us. Everyone went down into that shelter except one lady, whose husband was in the army. She would go hysterical every time the siren went and she never wanted to go into the shelter. They used to have to carry her down. I used to like going into the shelter, because we used to have puddings and things.

Dorothy Knowles

Watching the flying death

I can remember the first flying bomb, doodlebug, coming over Oldham. It were on a weekend; we were in the back and we heard this 'zzzzzzz' coming over. My father said, 'It's a flying bomb!' We all ran outside to have a look and we actually saw it going towards Abbey Hills. Then all of a sudden the engine cut out and there was this awful silence. My father rushed us all down to the cellar.

William Turner

The soldier's return

I often appeared in pantomimes, along with another girl called Marjorie Bradbury. We were once in 'Jack and the Beanstalk'. It was during the war and Marjorie's husband had been away for three years. Marjorie was climb-

Top left: Sheila Parsons (Shipp), Salvage Queen, 1941.

Top right: An Oldham Parish Church Rose Queen procession in the late 1930s. Sheila Parsons (Shipp) is lady-in-waiting at the Queen's left.

Above left: Sheila Parsons (Cinderella) and Marjorie Bradbury (Prince Charming).

Above right: Sheila Parsons (Shipp), Salvage Queen, with Tom Heap (Lord Mayor), Alan Findlater (Town Clerk) and Beryl Watson (left) Dorothy Rool (right).

Women share a joke, despite the mayhem caused by bombing.

ing the beanstalk, which her father had made. While she was climbing her husband, home on leave, appeared. He was waiting when she came down and he picked her up and swung her around in his arms.

Marian Hesketh

able to march. The captain who was doing the intake when I went in the army said, 'What do you do for your daily job, Hoyle?' I told him I was a butcher. 'Right,' he said, 'signals will do for you.'

Ronald Hoyle

Army Logic

When I was born they had thought I would never survive. When the Second World War started, my brother and I had to go for medicals. My mother and father said, 'Don't worry, Ron, they'll never take you. They'll take your brother though, he's as fit as a fiddle.' In actual fact they passed me, but didn't pass my brother. They said he had flat feet and wouldn't be

God Will Watch

My husband was killed in the Second World War and my mother was staying with me in Hawksley Street, which was a long street. We used to shelter under the stairs if there was a raid and we also had to put a sandbag outside the door. One night there was a bombing raid on Manchester and I had forgotten to put the sandbag out so my mother went to do it. My son was three and I had a twenty-month-old baby. I thought she would need help, so I put the baby on the table. When I came back in, she was just rolling off the table and I managed to catch her. 'Don't worry,' I said to my mother. 'God knows that I have had enough and he will not let anything happen to this house. We will be perfectly safe.' The last three houses in the street got a direct hit; every other house in the street had either a cracked or a smashed window. One poor man was killed when the bomb hit. My house didn't suffer any damage at all.

Mary Timms

Prisoners of War

I can remember the doodle-bug crashing on Abbey Hills. I was living in Greenacres at the time, only about a mile away from Abbey Hills as the crow flies. The bed was bouncing when the doodle-bug exploded. The weapon made a very distinctive sound, I remember. There was a

Right: Workers clear up at Abbeyhills.

Below: Volunteers sift through the wreckage in Oak Road.

prisoner-of-war camp in a mill at the bottom of Wellihole Street. The prisoners had to work, and we were told they were starving. Someone brought a loaf of bread and I can remember hanging over this wall and handing it to the prisoners. I used to watch the prisoners being marched down Lees Road. Some American soldiers guarded them once.

Derek Lloyd

A Little Girl's Terror

During the war the siren used to be on at Werneth Mill, straight across from our house. I could see the actual machinery of the siren from the door of my parents' shop. When the siren sounded, it was very menacing for a little girl like me. The sound started low down and it used to build up until it was really horrendous. We had a roll-top desk with a space for your knees, and I used to hide in there when the siren went. I remember the doodle-bug that came over Abbey Hills. Mum said, 'As long as we can hear it, we are safe.' Then it suddenly went silent and fell on Abbey Hills.

Phyllis Thomson

A Wartime Romance

I worked at the Royal Navy Stores all through the war. I met my future husband while I was there. He came from Liverpool and he was stationed at the Elm Mill, just down the road. He was only there for two and a half weeks and then he was sent abroad. For the next four and a half years we corresponded; writing and writing all the time. He came home in 1945 on a month's leave. He spent two weeks with his parents in Liverpool and I stayed with him there. We got engaged and then he had to go back to Italy. He stayed there until 1946, and we got married in June of that year. We had only seen each other for perhaps five weeks since we met. Eventually we came back to Oldham to live with my mum and dad, because he couldn't get a job in Liverpool. We lived with them until we could afford to get a little house, one-up, one-down, in Back Turner Street, off Manchester Road. It was 7s 6d a week.

Emily Smith

seven

Leisure and Entertainment

Robson Street looking towards Union Street.

Ashton Road in the 1930s

Ashton Road was full of shops, right from Hathershaw School up to the Star Inn. There were little terraced houses dotted in between. The left hand side, going towards Ashton, was full of shops, all different kinds. There was one of everything but, over the years, they have all disappeared. I used to go with my mum when she went into Oldham shopping on Friday nights. She used to go on a Friday night to get a piece of meat cheaply for Sunday dinner. The butchers sold the meat off because they had no fridges. She used to put the meat – and our milk – on a marble slab in the pantry to keep it cool.

Emily Smith

Shopping around Rhodes Bank

Beever Street, where I lived as a child, stretched from Rhodes Bank up to Egerton Street. There was good shopping around there. You could go to the bottom of Beever Street and you could shop from Hill's Stores, which was quite a way up the main road going out of Oldham, down to Mumps Bridge. Grafton House was a good shop for blouses and dresses and there was a lovely shop called Buckley and Prockter's. That was at Mumps Bridge. You only went there if you had plenty of money. I used to walk home from work and look in the windows. I once saved my money up to buy a coat from there.

Dorothy Bennett

Saturday morning in Robson Street

At the top of Robson Street, where I lived as a girl, there used to be a delicatessen. My mum used to send me there every Saturday for bacon and whatever else she needed. There was a little street with a sweet shop, and Dawson's, a dress shop, at the end. Then there was Bridge Street and the Odeon cinema. Across the road there was a little street called Bow Street, where there was a butcher's and a place where you took your radio battery for charging. I used to go to a pork shop and to Burney's for a cottage loaf and a cake called a Russian Sandwich. Then I'd go next door to Ramsden's for ham. If I had time I would have to pay for the papers. That was my Saturday morning.

Dorothy Knowles

A screaming baby

Gregory's was a place where you could have pudding 'n' chips. My mum worked there for a while. I once knew a lady who had a baby daughter who was always screaming. She used to go to Gregory's and this baby would be screaming outside and everybody would be asking, 'Whose baby is it?' She used to ignore it. 'I have it all day,' she'd say. 'I'm having my pudding 'n' chips.' The milliner's, Hardcastle's, was next door to Woolworths. They used to sell all sorts, stockings and gloves and upstairs was for clothes. It was quite an upmarket place. I worked in Woolworths on a Saturday, when I was a teenager. They moved us around from counter to counter. All the lads used to come in you'd see when you went dancing. It felt right posh.

Dorothy Knowles

The black pudding lady

They used to have the Wakes on Oldham market. They must have moved all the stalls to the sides. On Friday night we would collect up all the bottles we could and take them back to the shops to get our pennies to go to the Wakes. They had all sorts on the Wakes, roundabouts, horses, a waltzer and lots of stalls like the one where you rolled your penny down. There used to be a lady on the Wakes with black puddings. She was a very big lady and she used to have this big tub – they were nearly as wide as each other. The tub was full of black puddings. They were gorgeous.

Dorothy Knowles

Fabulous Oldham Wakes

When Oldham Wakes was on the market ground – two weeks in June, I think – the fairground people used to come from miles away. They shifted all the market stalls and the first thing you saw as you came up towards the market ground was the Dragons. In the middle there was nothing but roundabouts and there were sideshows running all round the market – boxing, fat women, thin women, etc. Everything used to shut down for Oldham Wakes; all the cotton mills used to close for two weeks.

William Turner

The Brownies and Essie Birch

We belonged to a little gospel mission in Peel Street. It was a very friendly place. I joined the Brownies and we had a Brown Owl called Essie Birch. She was absolutely great. Her mother was a dressmaker and Essie wrote pantomimes for the Brownies to perform. I was Snow White in the first one and Lord Dandini in another.

Lily Radcliffe

Oldham Wakes.

Oldham Wakes charabanc trip to Blackpool, 1931.

Having fun in the forties

I had a good time in my young days. Monday night it was the Palladium cinema. Tuesday night I'd go to friends and we'd all wash us hair. Wednesday night we stayed in. Thursday night were bath night. We'd go to Central Baths and then across the road for pudding and mash. Friday night we'd go to Savoy, dancing. Saturday night it were Savoy, Majestic and King Street Stores. Then we started going to Blackpool. The train left Oldham at 4.00 p.m. on Saturday. For half a crown you could get to Blackpool and into the Tower for dancing. All you needed were twopence for a wash and sixpence for an 'Oh be joyful' drink – a small bottle of beer. The train used to get back to Oldham about 3.00 a.m. You could walk home alone and had nothing to fear.

Elsie Turner

The Blackpool Express

There were quite a few dance halls in Oldham. One, at the top of Manchester Street, was called the Top Drum and there was a coloured man who played the drums. On Saturdays a special train used to run to Blackpool. It started off at Mumps. More often than not we used to get it at Werneth Station on Featherstall Road. We had a night out in Blackpool, at the Tower or the Winter Gardens, dancing and drinking. I think the train used to start back about midnight. It seemed to take ages coming back because they used to put it in sidings for express trains to pass. We used to get home about three or four o'clock in the morning. The train ticket included admission to Blackpool Tower.

Brian Bardsley

Queuing up

The cinema was so popular in the thirties and forties that you couldn't just walk in; you had to queue up. You went early, so that you would be near the front of the queue. The doorman would walk along the queue announcing 'Two single seats'. If you were with a boyfriend, you wanted to sit together. When I was younger, if it was an adult picture and children had to be accompanied by an adult, we would look for some likely person in the queue and say plaintively, 'Will you take me in Mrs?' It was nearly always a woman we asked!

Marian Buckley

Dracula's got you

I remember going to the pictures once when I was courting. It was the Empire, I think. We had had the news and the little picture. There were two girls sitting in front of us. Some boys came in and sat either side of these girls. The big picture started. It was *Dracula*. Part way through the film, just as Dracula was making one of his appearances, one of the boys, who had an umbrella, hooked the handle around one of the girl's necks. Her scream was better than any that we heard from the screen. Perhaps she will read this and remember.

Dorothy Bennett

Things to come

My dad took me to see *Things to Come*, in the Odeon I think. At the end of the film, they are off to the moon and, as we were coming out, I said to dad, 'Do you think they'll get to the moon?' He looked at me and said, 'In your lifetime Winnie, but not in mine'. When *Gone with the Wind* came to the Palladium a crowd of us went from work to see it. There was torrential rain. The cinema had a kind of glass cover to shelter the people who were queuing up, but the cover had sprung a leak. We were all totally soaked. We watched *Gone with the Wind* with our shoes off.

Winnie Maiden

ODEON
OLDHAM

Telephone: MAIn 1928.

Continuous: 2-0 to 11.

MONDAY, OCTOBER 5th, for Six Days Only—

H. G. WELLS'
GREATEST MASTERPIECE,

"THINGS TO COME" (Cert. 'A.')

SHOWING DAILY at 2-0, 4-15, 6-30 and 8-15.

Also GAUMONT BRITISH NEWS, &c., &c.

DEAF AIDS SUPPLIED FREE. Apply, Box Office.

PRICES OF ADMISSION: 6d. to 1/8. MATINEE: 6d. and 1/-.

Advert for Odeon showing Things to Come.

GEM
SUPER CINEMA,
Tel. MAI 1920, WERNETH.

General Manager: H. V. JACKSON

Monday to Friday. Continuous from 6-2 Saturday (Two Houses) 6-20 and 8-30.

MONDAY, OCTOBER 5th, for Three Days—

KAY JOHNSON, with IAN HUNTER, in

"JALNA"

(Cert. 'A.') Also CAROL COOMBE and CYRIL CHOSACK in

"THE MAN WITHOUT A FACE"
(Cert. 'A.')

THURSDAY, OCTOBER 8th, for Three Days—

LILY PONS in

"I DREAM TOO MUCH"
(Cert. 'U.') with HENRY FONDA, ERIC BLORE and OSGOOD PERKINS.

LA SCALA, GREGORY STREET, HOLLINWOOD.

ALL NEXT WEEK:

SHIRLEY TEMPLE and JOHN BOLES in
"THE LITTLEST REBEL" (U.)

Special Children's Matinee, Saturday, at 2 o'clock. Admission 2d. and 3d.

Advertisements for the Gem and La Scala cinemas.

Talkies

I can remember the first talkie coming to Oldham. I was fourteen and had just started work when the Grosvenor cinema showed *The Singing Fool*, with Al Jolson. We couldn't afford to go. But near Hawksleigh Street we had the La Scala cinema. I saw that being built. Seats cost 3d, 6d and 9d. We used to go twice a week. The Gem was on the border of Chadderton and Hollinwood, where the Gem Mill was. The first time my husband came home on leave from the army, we went to the Roxy at Hollinwood, which was originally going to be called the Regal.

Mary Timms

Getting lost in La Scala

La Scala was in a poor area, just off Manchester Road; the cinema was a bit run down in many ways, but I loved to go there. They used to change the film on Mondays and Thursdays. On Monday it was 7d, but on Tuesday and Wednesday you could get in for 4d, only you had to sit on the front row, if you were not accompanied by an adult. On Thursday it was 7d, 4d on Friday and 7d again on Saturday. La Scala didn't show the big films, which went to the Odeon and Gaumont, but for 4d I could go there and get lost for two hours.

Ernest Walker

Losing my way

I have never had any sense of direction. I had once been to the Roxy in Hollinwood to see *September Affair*, a lovely romantic film, which starred Joan Fontaine and Joseph Cotten. I came out of the cinema humming the beautiful 'September Song', went to get the tram home and got on the wrong one, to find myself going into Manchester.

Ella Lloyd

Manners

We used to sit in the back row of the Gem cinema, which was flea-ridden. You couldn't sit still in it. I didn't go to the cinema often, but I do remember the first time I was going out with my future husband. We had arranged to meet outside the Roxy in Hollinwood. I decided not to go. My mum said, 'I thought you were going out'. 'No, I'm not going', I said. She was very angry. 'You are not leaving that boy outside that cinema. If you are not going out with him, you are going down there to tell him'. I went, and I said, 'I'm not staying'. He was gentleman enough to walk all the way from Hollinwood back up to Werneth with me, to see me home safely.

Phyllis Thomson

Tea and double seats

The Victory cinema on Union Street used to show the Shirley Temple films, which I loved. The building is still there, though derelict now. The King's cinema – and that building also survives – was opposite the Coliseum. The King's had a lovely cafeteria. The women who worked there always had nice little black dresses or a skirt with a black top and a little pinny and a cap. It was a big treat to go to the King's for something to eat. You didn't have to go to the cinema; you could just have a meal. There were double seats in the King's for the courting couples.

Meryl Taylor

Ever been had?

I had a Saturday job on Tommyfield Market when I was fifteen. A whole bunch of us used to go to the pictures together. We'd meet when we had finished on a Saturday and go off to the first house on Saturday night. We'd all get something to eat and we would be sitting fourteen or fifteen in a row. We sometimes went to the Victory, which had a reputation as a fleapit. I once went there with a friend named Nobbie Nolan. The Victory had, by then, begun to show films that were a little risqué. One particular Saturday they billed what they called a 'torrid French picture'. It was called, *The Fruit is Ripe*. Nobbie and I went along, trying to look a lot older than we were. They let us in and it was a film about ... the grape harvest.

Michael Mills

Standing Room Only

We used to go to the King's cinema, where they had a restaurant. Oldham Parish Church used to hold their 'Bring and Buy' and their 'American Tea' in there. The Victory and the Grosvenor were both old buildings. I loved the Gaumont because they had an organ which

The King's cinema.

was played before the film started. More often than not we had to queue up for the cinema and in all weathers. Sometimes we would get a notice saying 'Standing Room Only'. Other times we would ask how long the wait would be. We might be told half an hour, so we would move on to some other cinema.

Sheila Shipp

Troublemaker?

When we were kids and teenagers we used to go to the pictures a lot. We always had to queue, sometimes for a very long time. But the films that we saw took us into a world of romance, excitement and luxury, a world we would never know. We always got two films for our money. We used to go to the Savoy cinema, which was opposite Hill's Stores. There were steps leading up to the entrance. Derek always looked very young. The manager was, we all thought, very officious and very nasty. One night, while we were queuing, somebody pushed Derek. He pushed them back. The manager got Derek by the scruff of his neck, called him a troublemaker and threw him down the steps. He landed at the feet of a policeman, who simply said the manager was within his rights. Poor Derek had done nowt!

Ella Lloyd

A sticky situation

My mum, dad and I used to go to a little cinema on Huddersfield Road. It was a very small place; even if you sat at the back you were too near the front. Mum was crippled with arthritis. One night she said to me, 'I've dropped my glove. Pick it up'. I couldn't. 'Jim, I've dropped my glove. Pick it up'. 'I can't' 'Why?' 'I'm stuck'. 'How do you mean, you're stuck?' 'I'm sitting on a piece of chewing gum', dad hissed. The film ended and they

Advertisement for the Savoy cinema.

Advertisement for the Cosy cinema.

played the National Anthem. Everyone stood up − except dad. 'Go for the manager, Joyce'. The manager was one of these figures round from every direction, red face and exceedingly large red nose. He said he was busy. Dad pulled away at his trousers and eventually managed to separate himself from the seat. He marched up to the manager, pointed at his backside and said, 'What are you going to do about this?' Mum had one of her giggling fits and we fled to a shop doorway a few doors away. Then she said, 'I really ought to be there, helping your dad'. We went back. There was my dad, bent double; his coat pulled up. The fat manager had a bottle and some cotton wool and was dabbing away at dad's backside. My mother was in hysterics and dad never forgave her for not sticking up for him.

Joyce Mills

The Cosy

Because I lived on Robson Street I could practically fall out of bed and into any of the Oldham town centre cinemas. There was the Odeon, the Palladium, the Gaumont, the Victory, the Grosvenor, the King's, the Electraceum and the little Cosy. I never went to the Electraceum, which I believe became a dancehall eventually. The Cosy was on Roscoe

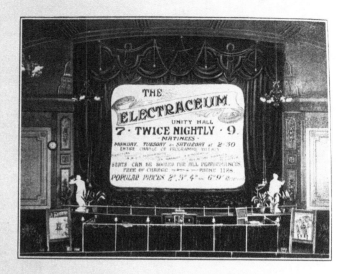

THE ELECTRACEUM

Oldham's Leading Picture House.

We ~ Attract, ... Fascinate, . . and Satisfy.

✦

TWICE NIGHTLY, 7 and 9.

MATINEES:
Mon., Tues., Sat., at 2-30.

ONLY at the ELECTRACEUM is the . . . Biggest, Brightest & Best Programme.

Advertisement for the Electraceum cinema.

Street, with its entrance on Bridge Street. My aunty and I used to go there every Friday. She would be wearing her shawl and I'd be toddling along beside her. All the seats there were 2d, but the row at the back was raised and it was 3d to sit there. We used to go on Saturday afternoons as well.

Dorothy Knowles

Where's the baby?

The Electraceum was one of the oldest cinemas in Oldham. My mother and father went there a lot. They once took me there when I was only a baby. They lost me and had to have a real search for me before they found me crawling under the seats.

Marian Hesketh

Fleapits and picture palaces

The first cinema I went to was the Alhambra, on Horsedge Street, higher up than the Theatre Royal. We used to sit on forms. On Saturdays we'd get a penny and we'd buy one of them spearmint bars as we went in. The Alhambra was a bug hut. You came out right at the side of Cook's Funeral Directors. The Alhambra was owned by a man called Shaw, who also owned the Cosy on Bridge Street. Another bug hut was the Electraceum facing the Antelope Pub. The Gaumont was a palace; Fenner used to play the organ there and everyone sang. The Grosvenor on Union Street was a very impressive building.

Stuart McDonough

The Gaumont – note the poster 'Fenner at the Wurlitzer'.

Singing with Fenner

We loved to go to the Gaumont. They had a cinema organ and a man named Fenner used to play at each performance. He would play the organ, they would put the words up on the screen and everybody would sing. Once or twice, because he knew that Marian had been in pantomimes, he would invite her to go up and sing.

Jim Hesketh

Not a place to visit?

Among the many cinemas in Oldham was the Cosy. It was just a little cinema and one you were not supposed to go to. If your mother knew that you'd gone there, there'd be trouble. I only went there once. I remember being given an orange as I went in. People used to say, 'If you go to the Cosy, don't sit on the front row. The boys at the back don't bother to go to the toilets and they wee there and it all runs down to the front!'

Marian Hesketh

Stop the noise

I sometimes on a Sunday night went to the Electraceum. There would be about twenty of us. It was really dark. We would walk in, whispering loudly 'Where are you?' All these voices would shout out, 'Shut up!' and threaten to throw you out if you didn't stop making a noise. It was a bit of a fleapit. So was the Cosy, where you had to sit on boxes.

Kathleen John

Cinemas in Chadderton

I often went to the Lyric cinema, in Milne Street, because it wasn't far from where I lived. It was 1d to go in the stalls and 2d to sit

LYRIC CINEMA

MILNE ST. CHADDERTON

MONDAY, TUESDAY, WEDNESDAY
Montgommery Clift, Paul Douglas
in " THE BIG LIFT " (A)

THURSDAY, FRIDAY, SATURDAY
Wayne Morris, Janis Paige
in " THE YOUNGER BROTHERS " (A)
Also " ONE LAST FLING " (A)

Advertisement for the Lyric cinema, Chadderton.

upstairs. I used to collect empty jam-jars and take them back to the Co-op, and they would give you money for them. I used to like to sit upstairs in the Lyric because it seemed a bit posher. Sometimes I would go to the Casino which was on Neville Street.

Lily Radcliffe

'Frank, are you there?'

I was only a little girl when the war was on, and we had the blackouts. My mum and I used to go to the pictures a lot, especially to the Odeon, which was very near where we lived. The first time we went out in the blackout, it was pitch black, with no lights at all. My mum kept saying, 'Frank, are you there?' 'Mum', I said, 'why do you keep saying that?' 'So they will think there's a man with us', she said, and no-one will come near. We couldn't see each other, let alone anyone else, but it got to be a game. 'Are you there?' she'd say. And I'd answer, 'Yes, he's here'.

Dorothy Knowles

In the mood for dancing

I loved to go dancing at Billington's. While I was going there frequently the most popular song was Kay Starr's 'Wheel of Fortune'. Later I went to the Savoy, where Tommy Smith and his Dance Band played. He had three singers, Terry Di Costa, Jerry Brereton, who was blind, and Joe King. They were all very good and we had some lovely times. We used to do waltz, quickstep, etc and jive, and when the band took half an hour's break, they used to play records for us to dance to.

Meryl Taylor

Mr Billington and the cakes

We used to go dancing at Billington's, which was on Ashcroft Street. It was run by Albert Billington and his wife. I worked in the offices of Granville Woods, Manufacturing Chemists, which were opposite Billington's, so we used to be able to see the Billingtons teaching dancing. A little van used to come to Billington's with cakes, and Albert would always leave me one on top of his car. He'd say,

The ABC cinema, formerly the Palladium.

The Palladium (later ABC) cinema.

'Come over sometime, and I'll teach you the tango'. I think it was because I was very dark when I was a girl. I remember going to the food office during the war and they pointed me to the queue for foreigners. I think they thought I was Spanish because I was so dark ... and I'd only gone for food coupons for my little sister.

Marian Hesketh

Let's go to Billington's

Billington's had two floors. There were poles which probably supported the upstairs. We used to say that it was common downstairs.

SAVOY
SUPER BALLROOM.
XMAS GREETING to All at Home and Abroad.
DANCING TONIGHT.
To Slap Happy
TOMMY SMITH'S
PERFECT TEMPO
SWING BAND.
ONLY 1/6 TONIGHT.
Dancing Every Night Except Wednesday.
For Your Xmas Ticket.
Box Office Open 11 to 4.
A FEW LEFT.
Xmas Day, Boxing Day Tickets.

TEL. MAI. 5500.
Majestic Ballroom
SATURDAY NEXT
GRAND XMAS CARNIVAL
Novelties, Competitions, Free Gifts.
Carnival Hats, &c., &c.
LATE DANCING
ADMISSION 5/- ADMISSION.
XMAS DAY, DANCING
BOXING DAY—LATE DANCING.
TUESDAY EVENING AS USUAL.

Advertisement for Savoy and Majestic ballrooms.

I don't know why, but I would never go downstairs. Once you had gone in, the girls couldn't go out, but boys could get a pass-out. There used to be a bloke called Frank on the door. If there was nobody about, he would say, 'Go on, you can go in', and he'd let one or two of us in for nothing. Mind you, we were never away; he probably thought we lived there. As you went in, you walked across the floor and there was a cloakroom with a line of mirrors. All the girls would be stood inside combing their hair. The girls would buy leg tan from a chemist called Braddock and Bagshaw. It was a powder and you could wear it for two days. But on the second day the powder would be all over the sheets of your bed and your mother went mad. One Saturday night it was raining, so I wore my wellingtons to the dance hall. When I took them off, they had taken the powder off, and I had a ring around my legs.

Dorothy Knowles

Vanity, thy name is woman!

When stockings were difficult to get, girls used to paint their legs. I didn't do that very much. I remember once I had a pair of stockings on, and, because I was quite tall, they didn't come far enough up my legs. So I could only fasten the front suspender. I was going down the steps at the Empire and one of the suspenders gave way. Further down, the other one went. I had to go to the toilet and take the stockings off. I had thought I was so dressed up when I put them on!

Dorothy Bennett

Dancing at the Majestic

When I was a teenager, I went dancing three or four times a week at the Majestic. It was on Bloom Street, off Manchester Street. There were lots of dance places, but Majestic was my

Miss Cook's Juvenile Players, *c.* 1937. Marian Knowles (Hesketh) is second from left in the front row.

The Children's Centenary Show at the Empire Theatre, 1949.

Empire Theatre interior.

favourite. It was one of the biggest ballrooms and you met some lovely people. On Thursday night it was 1s 6d to get in; Friday it was 2s; Saturday it was 2s 6d; Sunday night it was 2s again. The Majestic had its own resident orchestra and they used to have all the big ballroom dances there.

Kathleen John

The Chicken Run

When I was a teenager in the late 1920s and early 1930s, I used to go dancing at the Savoy, Hill's Stores and a place called the Castle. My mother always used to say, 'Think on. You are in by such and such a time'. I was always late and I'd go flying across Lees Street and she'd be standing on the door saying, 'Come on! Come

on!' Queen's Road, at the side of Alexandra Park, was known as the Chicken Run. Fellers and girls would be parading up and down showing off and looking for girl or boyfriends. Union Street was the same. Once I remember going to the Empire Theatre. Joseph Locke, the Irish singer, was starring there and he said, 'Look at this lady on the front row with the lovely hat'. The lady were me!

Lillian Wood

Carnivals and Whit Walks

Oldham Carnival was held in the summer and everyone joined in. It was held for charity. The carnival used to come along Gas Street one way and Union Street the other, and I think it ended up at Alexandra Park. We had the Whit

EMPIRE THEATRE
OLDHAM

General Manager:
R. MORECAMBE

Telephone:
MAIN 4362

Commencing Saturday, Dec. 23 to Saturday, Jan. 6, 1968

PLEASE NOTE TIMES OF PERFORMANCES

SATURDAY, DEC. 23rd ... 5 p.m. and 8 p.m.	MONDAY, JAN. 1st ... ... 2.15 and 7.15
MONDAY, DEC. 25th ... THEATRE CLOSED	TUESDAY, JAN. 2nd ... ... 2.15 and 7.15
TUESDAY, DEC. 26th ... 2 p.m., 5 p.m., 8 p.m.	WEDNESDAY, JAN. 3rd ... ... 2.15 and 7.15
WEDNESDAY, DEC. 27th ... ... 2.15 and 7.15	THURSDAY, JAN. 4th... ... ... 2.15 and 7.15
THURSDAY, DEC. 28th ... ... 2.15 and 7.15	FRIDAY, JAN. 5th ... ... 2.15 and 7.15
FRIDAY, DEC. 29th ... ... 2.15 and 7.15	SATURDAY, JAN. 6th ... 2 p.m., 5 p.m., 8 p.m.
SATURDAY, DEC. 30th ... 2 p.m., 5 p.m., 8 p.m.	

Philip Bernard presents a traditional "Laughter-Package" Pantomime

ON THE STAGE

WITH GUEST STAR

JOSEF LOCKE
IN
MOTHER GOOSE

WITH

FROM "OPPORTUNITY KNOCKS"
BOBBY BENNETT
TOP T.V. IMPRESSIONIST

FROM RADIO CAROLINE NORTH
TONY PRINCE
OLDHAM'S OWN D-J

TWELVE REX GREY GIRLS	FRANK LYNN	SPEED MANIACS FILMED CAR RIDE

Avril Ellis ★ Betty Wood ★ Amanda Birkin

THE "I DON'T CARE" BOY
JOHNNY DALLAS
AS MOTHER GOOSE

PANTO DIRECTED BY AUBREY PHILLIPS AND PRODUCED BY JOSEF LOCKE

Popular Prices

ORCHESTRA STALLS ... ... 8/6 (Child 6/6)
CENTRE STALLS ... ... 6/6 (Child 5/–)
REAR STALLS ... ... 4/6 (Child 3/–)
CENTRE CIRCLE ... ... 8/6 (Child 6/6)
SIDE CIRCLE ... ... 6/6 (Child 5/–)
★ Child Prices NOT applicable Saturdays, Boxing Day or New Year's Day.

Party and Postal Bookings

O.A.P. PARTY RATES TO CERTAIN PER-FORMANCES: APPLY BOX OFFICE FOR DETAILS. PARTY AND POSTAL BOOK-INGS NOW ACCEPTED. THEATRE BOX OFFICE OPENS FROM NOVEMBER 13th ONWARDS FROM 10 A.M. TO 6 P.M.

Joseph Locke still appearing at the Empire Theatre in 1968.

Walks, when nearly every religious denomination walked at some point. They'd set off from their churches and congregate at the Star Inn or down at Mumps. On Sunday afternoons, when they had been dancing on Saturday night, everybody would congregate in Alexandra Park, walking up and down the parade and saying who they had seen on Saturday night.

Dorothy Knowles

Whit Walks, *c*. 1939 passing the entrance to Blue Coat School.

Whit Walks on Yorkshire Street, 1939.

Whit Walks in Manchester Street, *c*. 1947.

Oldham Carnival passing the Grosvenor cinema, 1958.

Whit Walks outside the Market Hall, 1938.

Above: The derelict Casino cinema.

Opposite, above: Oldham Carnival on Union Street, 1958.

Opposite, below: Oldham Carnival, 1937.

A teenage lad in the 1950s

There were three cinemas around where I lived – Casino on Palace Street/Neville Street, Imperial on Featherstall Road North and The Lyric in Chadderton. I went to the Casino often because the film changed twice a week. It was a large cinema, with a big circle. There were a lot of dance halls in Oldham and plenty of pubs. If you went in a pub then, you would say you were eighteen. 'Well, where do you work?' Then they gave you a real interrogation. I can remember taking part in the Whit Walks – getting dressed up in my best clothes, walking down Main Road, up Middleton Road, right up Featherstall Road, back to the church. I was also in the Cubs and Scouts and we went on church parade.

Tom Richmond

Teasing the spiritualists

I was born in 1910. Just below where I lived, in Busk Street, there was a large house. It was used as a spiritualists' meeting place. We used to get a drawing pin and fasten something to dangle over the window. We used to stay back and keep pulling whatever we had fastened so that it kept tapping on the window. We used to have a lot of fun.

Ralph Turner

Other local titles published by The History Press

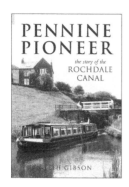

The Pennine Pioneer The Story of the Rochdale Canal
KEITH GIBSON

Rochdale Canal, the most successful of the three trans-Pennine canals, was built two hundred years ago. Trade boomed on the canal until the beginning of the twentieth century, when the arrival of motor transport had a dramatic effect on its importance as a trade route. It was formally abandoned in 1952. This book, which includes over 100 archive photographs, follows the life of the Rochdale Canal from its inception to its abandonment, and tells of the more recent battle for its restoration.

0 7524 3266 4

Gorton The Second Selection
JILL CRONIN AND FRANK RHODES

A collection of over 220 archive photographs, taking a look at some of the changes in leisure, housing, business and industry which have taken place over the last century in Gorton. A nostalgic look back at the pubs, cinemas, churches and schools that have changed over the years, including poignant photographs of VE Day street party celebrations. Each picture is supported by a wealth of historical detail sure to appeal to all who know, or have known, Gorton.

0 7524 2669 9

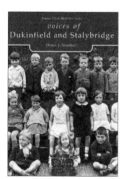

Voices of Dukinfield and Stalybridge
DEREK J. SOUTHALL

Oral history is unique in its facility to make the past accessible, and to catch the flavour of a time and the lives of the people concerned. This book combines vivid memories with the personal photographs of the interviewees, creating a valuable record of the first half of the twentieth century in and around this part of Greater Manchester. The reminiscences range from childhood games to first-time jobs, memories of war and anecdotes of local characters, such as the man with two birthdays, and the last tripe dresser in Stalybridge.

0 7524 2679 6

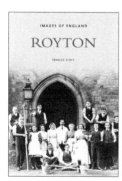

Royton
FRANCES STOTT

This collection of over 200 archive photographs traces the history of Royton as the town grew following the Industrial Revolution. Royton developed with the textile industry as mills and chimneys sprang up in the area during the Victorian era. This book explores the history of Royton, describing the people, pastimes, work and play of this busy community. The images will awaken nostalgic memories in people who have lived or worked in Royton, as well as providing a valuable resource for anybody interested in studying the history of the area.

0 7524 3516 7

If you are interested in purchasing other books published by The History Press, or in case you have difficulty finding any of our books in your local bookshop, you can also place orders directly through our website
www.thehistorypress.co.uk